No Limits

Developing Scientific Literacy Using Science Fiction

by

Julie E. Czerneda

Illustrated by Larry Stewart

Trifolium Books Inc.

Toronto, Canada

Reprinted from *Packing Fraction and Other Tales of Science & Imagination*, ed. Julie E. Czerneda
Trifolium Books Inc.

Packing Fraction © 1999 Charles Sheffield
Love is Chemistry © 1999 Jan Stirling
Changing Sex in MidOcean © 1999 Carolyn Clink
Much Slower than Light © 1991 Carolyn Clink
New Moon © 1997 Carolyn Clink
Stream of Consciousness © 1999 Robert J. Sawyer
Ancient Dreams © 1999 Josepha Sherman
Prospect Park © 1999 Julie E. Czerneda

Star Trek and associated names are trademarks of Paramount. *Babylon 5* is a trademark of Babylonian Productions. Other film and television titles/terms are trademarks of their respective production companies.

Trifolium Books Inc. acknowledges with gratitude the generous support of the Government of Canada's Book Publishing Industry Development Program (BPIDP).

Ordering Information
Canadian trade bookstores, wholesalers, individuals, organizations, and educational institutions: General Distribution Services, 325 Humber College Blvd., Etobicoke, ON, Canada M9W 7C3; Ontario & Quebec (800) 387-0141, local (416) 213-1919, all other provinces (800) 387-0172, FAX (416) 213-1917. Please contact Trifolium Books Inc. re: bulk purchases for educational, business, or promotional use.
U.S. orders: General Distribution Services (800) 805-1083

©1999 Trifolium Books Inc.
250 Merton Street, Suite 203,
Toronto Ontario M4S 1B1
(416) 483-7211; fax (416) 483-3533
trifoliu@ican.net
(http://www.pubcouncil.ca/trifolium)

Canadian Cataloguing in Publication Data
Czerneda, Julie E., 1955-
No limits: developing scientific literacy using science fiction
Includes index.
ISBN 1-895579-94-5
1. Science fiction — Study and teaching (Elementary). 2. Science fiction — Study and teaching (Secondary). 3. Science in literature — Study and teaching (Elementary). 4. Science in literature — Study and teaching (Secondary). 5. Literature and science — Study and teaching (Elementary). 6. Literature and science — Study and teaching (Secondary). I. Title
PN3433.7.C93 1999   809.3'8762'071   C98-932091-X

Editor: Julie E. Czerneda
Design/layout: Roger Czerneda
Illustrations: Larry Stewart
Cover Design: Fizzz Design Inc.
Project Coordinators: James A.W. Rogerson, Heidy Lawrance Associates

Printed and bound in Canada
10 9 8 7 6 5 4 3 2 1

What if...

Acknowledgments

I've never worked on a project that collected so much support and interest as it progressed, both from the teaching community and the science fiction community. It's been wonderful — though I'll say right now I can't imagine any one book living up to the expectations I've heard, no matter how long I work to perfect it! So to all of you who believe in innovative teaching and especially to those who share my love of science fiction, here's the result. May you find it a good, honest start at filling a need we all know exists.

When I started, I was definitely the new kid on the block (actually, I didn't even know the neighborhood!) and must sincerely thank those professionals who immediately believed in this project, contributing their talents and reputations so enthusiastically: Dr. Charles Sheffield, Josepha Sherman, Robert J. Sawyer, Jan Stirling, Larry Stewart, and Carolyn Clink. I'd also like to thank Nancy Kress for her interest and support (not to mention sharing Charles with me), as well as John Clute for permitting me to quote from his excellent resource.

I was fortunate to be in touch with several professionals already using science fiction in their teachings, and wish to thank these individuals in particular for their support and advice: Jeffrey A. Carver, Dr. David Degraff, David Brin, Pat York, Peter Lougheed, Mike McCann, Patti Simmons, Dick Edwards, Laurie Pfaff, and Fred Lerner (for last minute encouragement).

Special thanks to all those who read manuscript, providing helpful comments and suggestions: Jonathan Bocknek, Jennifer and Scott Czerneda, Roxanne Hubbard, Helen Yung, Robin Webster, Ava-Ann Allman, the students of Eastwood Collegiate, Collingwood Collegiate, Parkside High School, and Orillia District Collegiate Vocational Institute.

A special acknowledgement goes to the "Killer Bees." Authors Greg Benford, David Brin, and Greg Bear have been working tirelessly to promote science fiction in the classroom and to encourage scientific literacy. Their example has been an inspiration to me as I finished this project. Hope you like it!

Last, but not least, my thanks to all those at Trifolium Books who were willing to gamble I knew what I was doing and believe I would get it done. Thanks, Trudy, Jim, and Rodney!

"We especially need imagination in science. Question everything."

Maria Mitchell (1818-1889)
First woman to be professor of Astronomy at Vasser; only woman in the National Academy of Arts & Sciences until 1943.

Dedication

I dedicate this book to the ConComs of Toronto Trek, Ad Astra, Con*Cept/Boréal, STAO, and Bucconeer. These are the people who organize conventions, arranging every detail and ensuring all runs smoothly. These are also the people who have whole-heartedly embraced the use of science fiction in the classroom and who promote scientific literacy and a love of learning at every opportunity.

Thank you.

Other titles by Julie E. Czerneda

Science Fiction

A Thousand Words for Stranger (1997) DAW Books Inc.
Beholder's Eye (1998) DAW Books Inc.
Ties of Power (1999) DAW Books Inc.
Packing Fraction and Other Tales of Science and Imagination (1999) Trifolium Books Inc.

Science and Technology

Science texts and teacher resources published by John Wiley & Sons, D.C. Heath, and ITP Nelson
By Design (ed.) Trifolium Books Inc.
Take a Technowalk by Peter Williams and Saryl Jacobson (ed) Trifolium Books Inc.

Career Education

Career Connections Series (1994-1997) Trifolium Books Inc. & Weigl Educational Publishers:
Great Careers for People Interested in Living Things
Great Careers for People Who Like to Work with their Hands
Great Careers for People Interested in Communications Technology (with Victoria Vincent)
Teacher's Resource Banks I (with Dave Studd), *II* (with Caroline Toffolo), and *III* (with Susan Baker-Proud)

What if...

Table of Contents

lightening could be harvested and used for power?

Using No Limits

Science Fiction in the Classroom

Science fiction writers present their changed worlds in terms that are consistent with the language, the assumptions, and the arguments of contemporary science, or in terms that are consistent with our profound sense that human history is a continuous reality and that changes flow from what we know of that reality. Good SF says: if A is the case, it follows that B can happen."

John Clute, author of the *Illustrated Encyclopedia of Science Fiction*

The use and, indeed, acceptance of science fiction as a valid tool in teaching is very similar to the situation facing information technology. While most profess to knowing its value, there is often only one teacher in a department or school who is a true convert, acting as both expert and advocate. This person may be considered as an invaluable resource by many peers. At the same time, others may avoid this person and the crazy ideas he or she brings to school, perhaps hoping it's a mildly harmless phase that will go away with experience in the real world of classroom, budgets, and time. There is almost always at least one who speaks out in scornful dismissal, no matter how passionate the presentation or eloquent the proof.

Of course, neither slavish devotion nor scorn are helpful reactions. The teacher who knows and loves science fiction may have no idea how to adopt it as a useful resource for students. I've met many such people, wonderful educators, who confess they just want to have a chance to share their love of the genre with anyone and students, willing or not, are a captive audience. As for scorn, there will always be those who view the unfamiliar with hesitation and discomfort.

But just as information technology is permeating and enriching education, from curriculum to the list of Internet sites students talk about after class, so is this body of speculative literature, known as science fiction, beginning to take on a whole new relevance in today's classrooms. I hope you find this resource helps you use science fiction in a meaningful and enjoyable way with your students.

And if they develop a love of science fiction along the way, that's fine, too.

What is Scientific Literacy?

Consider literacy on its own for a moment. As a working definition, let's call literacy the ability to read with comprehension and purpose. A literate person is comfortable using words to communicate ideas and can critically interpret the communications of others.

Science is a process of inquiry and typically includes the body of knowledge produced by that inquiry.

Where do these concepts meet? Each and every time we are faced with information that is, or purports to be, scientific. So how do we "read" science, that is, evaluate it? Is it necessary to become scientists ourselves in order to understand today's increasingly technological and information-rich world? How do we critically interpret something that has resulted from a complex interaction of many types of knowledge and processes?

And, most importantly of all, how do we prepare our young people to live in a future where science will play an increasing role? By helping them become scientifically literate.

The Role of Science Fiction in Developing Scientific Literacy

Science fiction is story-telling that springs from one simple idea: *What if?* What if this or that scientific premise were different? What if things happened in a different order, or not at all? What if? For hundreds of years, science fiction has been a testing ground for scientific and social concepts — from those that have never existed to those we live with everyday.

This makes science fiction an excellent passageway to scientific literacy. When students read a good science fiction story, they are entertained. But as you guide them deeper into the science "what if" that lies beneath the story, they learn to explore scientific concepts with a critical eye, to see the importance of context and source, and to recognize potential issues.

In *No Limits*, you will find activities to help your students express their own "what if's" about science. Students will critically evaluate what they read about science topics and how science and scientists are portrayed. In so doing, they will take

Scientific Literacy: the knowledge and understanding of scientific concepts and processes required for personal decision making, participation in civic and cultural affairs, and economic productivity.

National Education Standards (1996) National Academy Press Washington

people could change the color of their skins at will?

Where to find it:
Use the worksheet, *Scientific Literacy Skills* (pg 115), to help students track their own progress.

Vocabulary

- Since an appreciation of the meaning of individual words is a key component of literacy, you will find vocabulary notes in the margins.
- Certain words have been defined on many of the worksheets in order to cue students to the particular usage being applied.
- It has been my experience that many students prefer to guess the meaning of words rather than ask. You may wish to start an ongoing list of words and their definitions on the bulletin board. Another approach is to challenge students to discover the meaning and correctly use a "word of the day."

Website This icon indicates a relevant Internet site.

The "What if..." on this page was explored by Nancy Kress in her acclaimed novel, *Beggars in Spain*.

important steps towards becoming scientifically literate, an essential accomplishment for both today and the future.

A scientifically literate person:

- identifies the scientific issues underlying personal and societal decisions.
- expresses their views on those issues in appropriate scientific terms.
- evaluates the quality of scientific information by considering both its source and the methods used to obtain this information.
- makes and evaluates arguments based on evidence and applies conclusions from such arguments appropriately.
- asks questions about what makes them curious in everyday life, and determines or finds the answers to those questions.
- reads and understands articles about science in the popular media, and discusses with peers the validity of their conclusions.
- distinguishes between what is and what is not a scientific idea.

An Overview of *No Limits*:

- Reproducible worksheets and lesson suggestions for using any science fiction with your students to develop creativity, critical reading skills, and an improved understanding of the role of science and scientists in society.
- Annotated versions of the original science fiction stories commissioned for *No Limits*. (These stories and verse are available for students in the anthology *Packing Fraction and Other Tales of Science and Imagination*, Trifolium Books Inc.)
- Reproducible worksheets and lesson suggestions for using the commissioned stories, poems, and illustrations.
- "Where to find it" tips to help you locate materials.
- Additional information about science fiction literature, authors, and other media.
- Creative writing tips and story suggestions throughout.
- Vocabulary assistance.
- Implementation tips based on classroom experience with these materials.
- Annotated Resource List, including recommended non-fiction print materials, films, fiction titles, and Internet websites.

What if...

Selecting Your Approach

I chose the title "No Limits" for two reasons. The first is the more obvious: that as literature, science fiction imposes no limits on creativity — on believability and rigor, yes — but never on the means, topic, or approach.

The second reason was my own observation that there really is no limit to how you can use science fiction in the classroom. I've provided only a sampling of the ways I've tried. Every time I speak to teachers, I find a new approach or application. It would surprise me if that didn't occur. Imagination begets imagination.

So, from a practical viewpoint, you need to select an approach, to decide what it is you want science fiction to help you and your students accomplish before you begin. Here are some of the criteria you may wish to consider:

Criteria

- Time allotted. Are you thinking in terms of a warmup activity to a unit of study or a project extending into 2 or more lessons?
- Type of evaluation and assessment preferred. The bulk of the activities in this book are based on a combination of participation and result.
- Is this an enhancement or part of core? While this definitely relates to time allotment, it is also an important point to consider when selecting the activities. If core, you will be dealing with a variety of reading abilities and interests as you work with the entire class. Many of the lessons in this book are geared to this variety. Watch for the group work icon.
- Is this to have a cross-curricular focus? If so, you may wish to involve the appropriate staff members in your planning.

Sources of Science Fiction: Print, Film, or Other Media

Science fiction has blossomed in every imaginable form, and, not surprisingly, makes up a majority of the new offerings in cutting-edge media such as gaming, virtual reality, and electronic publishing.

For the purposes of classroom use, however, there is still no more versatile and accessible format than the printed word. Science fiction works are found in the majority of school and

What if...
This is the underlying question of science fiction. ***What*** will happen to society, individuals, and/or the universe, *if* this aspect of science operates thus. It is the thrust that starts the speculation. From this point, the science within the story is as consistent with what is known as possible, within the realm of the story being told. You will encounter sample "What if's..." to help trigger your students' imaginations throughout this book.

"I use science fiction in my ...science courses to make abstract concepts more concrete, distant objects seem like real places, and to show the creative, imaginative side of science."

Dr. David DeGraff,
Professor of Astronomy,
Alfred University N.Y.

someone found a way to eliminate the need to sleep?

Where to find it:
There is an annotated list of recommended science fiction works-in-print at the end of this book. You will also find several websites which are devoted to identifying suitable works for student use. Both of these listings were developed using the following criteria:

- The work has a solid, identifiable scientific "what if" premise.
- The work is generally available.
- The content of the work would be considered by most educators to be accessible to student readers from 12 years and up.

In most groups, one or more students seem to take fire from ideas, leading both in how they express themselves and in their ability to inspire others. These are not always the individuals you'd predict. I remember one particularly articulate and passionate young man, whose comments were often so to the point and interesting the entire group hung on his every word. Each time he spoke, I had to glance at the teacher at the back of the room who'd pointed out this student to me before the session as someone who never uttered a word in class. She was smiling so broadly it's a wonder the students didn't pick up on it.

 This icon indicates activities that could be done at home.

public libraries. Many publishers keep even older science fiction works in print or else they can be found at second-hand bookstores. Given the vast amount of science fiction literature out there, the difficult aspect is selecting which to use. (See marginal note.)

This being said, a combination of film and print media can be extremely effective in reaching a class and quickly illustrating concepts such as world-building, plot, and pacing. I have listed some suggestions with specific Lessons. One recommendation I do have is to avoid the temptation to sit the class in front of an entire film. You will gain more by cueing up several short pieces of around 30 s each, and generating discussion between each. Then students can follow up by watching the films of interest on their own time. (See list of films, pg 122.)

Choosing an Appropriate Student Product

You will find as you read through the various lessons and activities that there is rarely only one possible product. This is because I've found it easier to tailor the end result to suit differing groups of students than to try and make the same project work for every situation. This flexibility means you can start any of the activities or lessons, but make your own decision where, and with which student product, you wish to end. You'll also note that I frequently suggest enlisting the class to make this and other choices. This is my style in the classroom and is only provided as a suggestion.

Points to consider when choosing the student product:

- Should the product be well-defined or open?
- What is involved (your time) in assessing the product?
- Do you wish to have group work or individual or both?
- Are there opportunities to have a product match other program goals?
- Which products best suit individual students?
- Can this product reasonably be done outside of class?
- Do you have the resources available to ensure student success with this product? For example, is there Internet access for students at your school? Will you need to arrange a trip to the public library in order to provide a sufficient variety of science fiction resources? (Hint: If you decide to supply books of your own to the class, be sure to keep careful track. Even if all are returned, be aware that paperbacks, especially those published in the last 15 years, tend to fall apart very easily.)

What if...

Implementing in the Classroom

There are tips on how to use the lessons and activities in class throughout this book, but there are a few basic concepts to be addressed for all.

Encouraging Creative Thought
Other than in classes devoted to writing skills development, most students need to warm up to the idea of thinking creatively in science. Be prepared for some resistance from those students who like everything "by the book." The "warm-up" icon marks activities you can use to get the class involved.

Group Dynamics
How well your class works as a unit, or in groups, will depend on two things: keeping the atmosphere non-critical and sharing expertise. A typical class contains only 1 - 5 % who admit to reading science fiction (include comics and gaming scenarios when you ask), and another 30 - 40 % who confess to following the X-files, Babylon 5, or other television series. I use "admit" and "confess" deliberately. Teenagers are very sensitive to the opinions of their peers and science fiction is often denounced as "kid's stuff" by teens and adults alike. I always find there is a moment after announcing you will be working with science fiction in the classroom in which you can tip the scales easily one way or another, towards interested acceptance or perceived ridicule. My only advice is this: you have to show the students that you yourself take science fiction seriously and that you will expect tolerance for all ideas and opinions.

The sharing of expertise has its own interesting potential pitfall. While groups should take advantage of expertise, you will likely find your worst class critics are the science fiction readers. Once they feel safe in the class, they will be the ones to trounce on the hesitant new ideas of the non-readers. It can be very tricky keeping these individuals satisfied without letting them turn off the rest of the students.

Worksheets and Lesson Suggestions
The worksheets in this book can be used with any science fiction material you prefer, including television and film. The lesson suggestions offer similar choices, but include activities based on the short stories from the student anthology, *Packing Fraction and Other Tales of Science and Imagination*.

Adding Excitement
Science fiction is supposed to be entertaining and (often) fun. Take advantage of this reputation to "jump-start" a reluctant or timid class. Come to class dressed as a mad scientist, then act normally. Surprise the students with posters and models around the room. Use props. (I have a great time with a 1 m T-rex model that roars.) I know of one teacher who comes to class in a Star Trek uniform on the first day of using science fiction. It's become an expected high point for students each year.

 This icon marks beginning or start-up activities.

Warm-up

Quick Index to Worksheets

something in the air caused printer's ink to fade away?

Recommended Materials:
- a selection of science-based headlines, ideally cut out and mounted on card stock for reuse.
- a can or box to hold the headlines
- Worksheet, *Lurid Headline Collection* (pg 10)
- Worksheet, *Short Story Plot Elements* (pg 11)

Recommended Student Product:
- a statement of the story concept, starting with "what if" premise and the consequence.
- a one-page plot outline
- a short story, 500 - 750 words (only if story-writing is a key element in your program.)

Warm-up

Where do ideas come from?
While the answer varies with each author, it's fair to say most science fiction authors are "information junkies" who read just about everything they can find, from science publications to newspapers to history texts. Many subscribe to Internet lists in order to learn more about topics of interest. Sometimes the most interesting ideas come from conversations. When Hubble telescope scientist Ingle Heyer led a group of sf writers on a tour of the Space Telescope image archive facility and described the robotic mechanism used to locate images for on-line requests, you could see the ideas sparkling in every set of eyes.

Using Science Fiction to Encourage Creativity in Science

The idea of being creative in science is unfamiliar to most students. The bulk of new information they are facing, the history underlying the scientific theories they investigate, even the precision of the instruments they use all conspire to make science in school seem immutable and solid. Yet one of the key aspects of the science is the interplay of creative and imaginative thought with observation and experiment. This flexibility is vital in order to interpret data in novel ways, to propose testable problems, and to push existing theories past what is momentarily accepted to new and more reliable explanations. Science is a human creative process as much as any art. (Throughout this book, you will find ways to help students examine this concept further.)

Science fiction is all about thinking beyond, about stretching the limits of what is known in science to what might be. The speculation of science fiction allows students to explore concepts, relationships, and potential societal impacts within their imaginations. So one of the single best uses of science fiction in any classroom, but particularly in science, is in the generation of story ideas based on scientific concepts.

How to Proceed
- If you wish, hand out the worksheet, ***Lurid Headline Collection*** (pg 10), a few days ahead of time to allow students to collect their own headlines to share with the class.
- Ask students "where science fiction writers obtain their ideas?" Record all responses. Point out that while most science fiction writers are not scientists, they share an interest in science concepts.
- Ask "what is the underlying question in science fiction?" Describe the questions in news accounts as "how, why, where, who" then lead to the science fiction premise of "**What if..**"

Modeling the Activity
- Choose a headline and write it where all students can see it. Explain to students that you will be using this headline as a starting point to generate a science fiction story as a class. Here is a sample of how to proceed. Note: the more enthusiasm you can bring to this stage of the activity, the better. It can take a second try at a headline to get students involved. Once

What if...

they grasp what to do, you may find the only problem is getting them to stop.

Eye in the Sky Foils Hawks

Here is a newspaper headline I've used with students. The article itself deals with technology used reduce the incidence of bird-plane collisions near an airport.

- The first step is to establish the "what if..." to be explored in the story. I give them a brief explanation of the article. Then I say, "let's change things a bit." As a class, we play with the content of the headline so it sounds more like science fiction. At this point, my purpose is to encourage them to speculate as freely as possible, not to take the science in this particular article and write directly from it.
- We start with "Hawk." I ask students to substitute something else. My preference is to have them call out their ideas, getting as noisy as possible. I then pick an interesting one or have the class choose. A simple hands -up voting system works well if there are multiple good ideas. In this case, the class agreed on "Aliens." It's typical to have fairly stereotypical, simplistic ideas to start with, until students have warmed up their creative thinking.
- For this headline, the change to "Alien" is enough to start. I ask the class to agree on the following parameters:
      Setting: on the Earth or off the Earth
      Time: Now, the Future, the Past
- They picked "on Earth" and the "Future." We refine the location (this can lead to some interesting twists), in this case: Australia; and the time period, in this case: a far distant future.
- Next, the class tosses around ideas about the "Eye in the Sky." Ideas range from "predatory cloud organism" to "a passenger arriving on a space ship." Any of the ideas could lead to interesting story possibilities. At this point some students are already half-writing their own stories. The class decides on a "Spy satellite."

Spy Satellite Foils Alien

- Now it's time to define the problem, to think creatively about the "what if..." in terms of a story's plot. I point out the word we haven't changed yet, "Foils" as indication of some unsuccessful effort by the alien. (In this case, the What if...revolves around an alien visiting Earth in the future.) This

Where to find it:
- Headlines - try the "Breakthrough" section of *Discover* Magazine; national newspapers, especially the science sections; news magazines which have science or technology features, such as *Time* Magazine.
- For the student's own headline search, I've also recommended the tabloids as these offer a great opportunity to investigate pseudo-science at the same time.

Accept anything the class accepts.
It is essential to establish a non-judgemental atmosphere during creative activities. At first, students, particularly the younger ones, are expecting you to censor them. When they realize you are not, you should notice a reduction in their other major anxiety, the opinion of their peers. It's worth allowing a bit of silliness to stir up their imaginations. Once they see you taking all ideas seriously, they should settle down.

Is it Science Fiction or Fantasy?
Depending on your class, you may need to distinguish between science fiction and fantasy in order to keep students writing what you wish. One quick demonstration is to show a dramatic illustration of a dragon. Ask the class to decide if a book with this image on the cover would be science fiction or fantasy. It can actually be either. A science fiction story about a dragon could be based on virtual reality, a robotic dragon, or other possibilities. A fantasy, on the other hand, would not provide a scientific rationale for the existence of a mythological creature and instead would rely on the existence of dragons as part of the world-building in the particular story.

television sets secretly transmitted images of viewers?

Record the class story elements where everyone can see them as each is determined during the open discussion.

Writing Assessment

Here is one way of breaking down your assessment of student writing:

Exceptional
- confidently integrates elements of writing
- creative and imaginative content

Solid Achievement
- control of elements of writing
- clear and complete content, not necessarily very original

Poor
- minimal to no grasp of writing elements
- unconnected, fragmented ideas

The Expert Witness

Ask students to name the expert witness - the character or device used to provide the essential scientific rationale or clues needed for the plot - in each of the different versions of Star Trek. Answers? Classic Trek: Mr. Spock; Star Trek: The Next Generation: Mr. Data; Star Trek DS9: a variety of characters, especially Dax and Dr. Bashir; Star Trek Voyager: a variety of characters, especially Torres and 7 of 9. The voice of the computer is also frequently used as an expert witness. (Star Trek names and titles are trademarks of Paramount.)

time, I gently discouraged ideas along the lines of "B-movie alien invasion" and waited for something more original to surface. Sure enough, the class decided the alien was on Earth to secretly harvest portions of the coral reef (the location <u>was</u> Australia). The spy satellites were there as monitors, so the people on Earth could prevent such thefts. I then asked the students why the aliens were stealing. The class decided the reef contained a substance the aliens needed to combat a fatal disease, but they couldn't meet Earth's price and were driven to theft.

- You can stop once students have created a scenario and proceed to repeat this exercise to this point with other headlines until you are confident they understand the process and can continue in their groups, but when time allows, I prefer to continue with the story elements of mood, protagonist, and expert witness.

Mood: Have the class concur on an overall mood to the story under construction: is it to be light and funny? dark and tragic? mysterious? etc. In my experience, most classes choose something between dark/ tragic and mysterious.

Protagonist: Given the form is a short story, there has to be a viewpoint character, through whom we experience what happens. I usually generate this character from the class by providing these choices and asking for a majority vote:
Human or Non-human (most classes pick human at first)
Male or Female (often leads to interesting class dynamics)
Age: less than 20, 20-30, 30-40, 40 and up (I note the class choice, often 20-30 the first time, and remind them there has to be something about this person which makes his or her ability to solve or understand the problem believable. There are usually some sheepish looks as they realize, for example, a world-renowned expert in nuclear physics is unlikely to be less than 20.)

Expert Witness: The character(s) or other vehicle the author uses to provide or interpret the required science in the story, particularly within space-limited media such as a short story or TV episode. Even in novel-length, it is very difficult to keep the story flowing well around chunks of expository text and most authors do their utmost to avoid the necessity. (One of the truly helpful things that students almost unfailingly do here is become so enraptured with the story-building process that their own stereotypical views of scientists — which they honestly don't realize they possess — come out. When I write the key words to describe the expert witness, then wait a

What if...

moment, you can hear the mental gears turning. Why did they make the expert witness a much older male? See page 20.)

- It generally takes less than five minutes to run through this the first time. Once students understand the process, it can take a little longer as more of them throw in ideas and the class debates different choices more fiercely. This is when you will need to shorten up discussion. You will also need to gently curb the enthusiasm of those students who would happily write an entire novel plot outline on the spot.

Proceeding with the Group Activity

- Once you are confident the class is ready, break them into their groups. Provide the worksheet, *Short Story Plot Elements* (pg 11) as a guide. Then let a member from each group draw a headline from the container. Tell them they can use the headline as is, or follow the pattern from the class story-building to modify the headline.

Group

- Allow ten minutes for the group to come up with a one-sentence description of their story concept based on the headline.

- After that time, have a member from each group read the headline, then describe their story concept.

- If you have time, the class can work on each of the story concepts to refine them further, by considering mood, protagonist, and expert witness.

Extension Opportunities

1. Creative writing: I've had an average of 3 students per class submit stories on their own following this activity, some to me but also some to their regular classroom teacher. To extend this into a full-fledged creative writing exercise, students could produce a completed story based on the beginnings done in class. They should be able to produce a complete and sufficiently complex work in under 750 words (approximately 3 pages double-spaced). This can be done as a group activity. Alternatively, offer it as a voluntary enrichment to those individuals interested in taking the story ideas further.

Group

Homework

2. Headline collection: Students can collect headlines and organize them by scientific "themes." This can be presented in the form of a scrapbook, poster, or even as part of a title page for a relevant science activity.

Warm-up

Recommended Story-writing Guidelines:

- Allow one "what if..." extrapolation, that is, one creative leap from what is known. From that point, all other science in the story must be believable in terms of what the student knows of real science. For example, allow the premise "what if the humming of tires on a new kind of pavement caused people to become easily enraged." From that point, cars and people should "behave" the way science currently postulates.

- Accept all ideas as equally valid during the creative building of the story.

- If you are finding it difficult to assess students in terms of participation during this activity, use smaller groups with more defined responsibilities. One approach is to divide the story elements among the group members.

- Encourage students who are submitting stories to work through more than one draft of their work. While creativity within a science fiction theme is the target, writing is a craft which benefits from practice and appropriate criticism.

Many science fiction authors attend science fiction conventions in which they participate in panel discussions on any number of topics of interest to fans and their own peers. The "Green Room" is where panelists relax before they appear, and it's traditional for the Green Room to offer beverages, snacks, and a collection of the latest supermarket tabloids. Why the tabloids? Suffice it to say that nothing starts a hilarious conversation among science fiction authors faster than the wilder claims of such publications.

rain-making technology was sold in local stores?

Lurid Headline Collection

Have you ever stared at a blank page or screen, wondering what on earth to write? Has a good story idea seemed as hard to find as free time? Fear not! In science fiction, ideas can jump right out of the daily headlines.
(Free time, well, not so easy.)

1. Start your own collection of headlines. They can come from any source — "those" magazines at the grocery store, the local paper, or even from television — as long as they have something to do with science.

2. Record the headline, where you found it (source), and when.

3. Then, when you are ready to write, check over your collection for some unusual starting ideas.

Headline	Source	When

lurid: def'n. sensational, horrifying, or terrible (lurid details); vivid or glowing in color; showy, gaudy; revelation of facts or character in a horrific, sensational, or shocking way.

Short Story Plot Elements

Source (if any)
Record the headline or other source you are using to begin your plot construction.

What if?
What scientific idea will be explored by your story?

When will you set your story?
Now   Near Future   Far Future   Past

Where will you set your story?
On Earth?   Off Earth?

Any other details of setting? (For example, is it in your home town?)

What is the problem?
Based on your "What if?" decide the peril or difficulty your characters will face.

Who?

Who is/are your protagonists?

Who is the expert witness?

Who is/are the villain(s), if any?

Mood
Based on the problem and characters, decide what mood your story will have. For example, is it going to be funny or grim? (You may change your mind as you write.).

protagonist: def'n. the chief person in a story; the principal performer; the advocate or champion of a cause.

Using Science Fiction to Improve Critical Reading Skills

Recommended Materials:

- One or more science fiction short stories, either from *Packing Fraction & Other Tales of Science & Imagination* or another source.
- Selection of magazines containing popular science articles; ideally some which give information about their contributors, such as *Discover*, and some which give little or none, such as newspapers or *Time*.

Option A
- Worksheet *Beyond Mere Words I* (pg 16)
- Worksheet *Beyond Mere Words II* (pg 17)

Option B
- Worksheets *Short Story Analysis* (mount on card stock for reuse) (pg 18-9)

Recommended Student Product:

- a bulletin board of selected science articles, sorted by student criteria
- a critique of a science article or book feature
- a collection of articles and information about a particular science issue in the media
- a scientific story based on a "what if" premise concerning credibility
- a biography of a non-fiction science writer
- presentation on the career of a science writer/journalist
- a list of Internet sources of scientific information considered credible by the class as a whole
- a list of Internet sources of scientific information considered less than credible by the class as a whole
- a handout by students for students on how to evaluate sources of scientific information

In language arts, students are routinely involved in critical analysis of what they read. They learn about the author of a particular work, the societal context of when and where the work was written, and pay attention to any underlying meanings as well as the more obvious content.

When asked to research a science topic, these same students might check the copyright date on a text or library book. And in too many cases, that will be the extent of their critical analysis of what they are reading. Even more experienced students will absorb and treat as valid scientific information from sources as varied as journals to newspaper articles, from website postings to television documentaries.

If you want to see some bemused faces, ask your class to think about who writes their science books. It's something that simply hasn't occurred to them before. Have them read the copyright and acknowledgement pages. Discuss what's involved in a textbook. Emphasize that writing science is an activity performed by individuals, but usually for a publisher, (either in a business or institution), an organization or other group.

An excellent way to have students learn to critically read science, particularly popular science, is to start by having them analyze the authorship and content of a work of science fiction.

How to Proceed

Step I: Science Fiction

Choosing a science fiction story to read

I highly recommend using short stories for this type of assignment, for three reasons. First, the format forced the author to concentrate on the premise, the "what if..," making this type of writing the most accessible to analyze. Secondly, from a practical standpoint, students can read a 5000-word story and complete a related assignment in a fraction of the time a novel would take. Thirdly, it is easier (and cheaper) to obtain a variety of good short science fiction, especially newer works, than to provide the same quality and variety in full-length novels.

If you are using stories from the companion student anthology, *Packing Fraction and Other Tales of Science &*

What if...

Imagination, you can either let students choose the story that interests them, choose a story for the class that fits into the science topic currently (or upcoming) in your program, or choose a story based on the recommended reading level supplied with the stories in this resource.

While I've provided two sets of worksheets and approaches, feel free to use both in combination. For example, you can model story and article analysis for the class, using with the cards from Option B, then assign individual work with the ***Beyond Mere Words*** set as guides.

Option A - Individual Analysis
- Have students use the worksheet ***Beyond Mere Words I*** (pg 16) as a guide to analyzing their short story. Their predictions are important and should be as complete as possible before the research stage. This can be done in class or partially as a homework assignment.

Homework

Option B - In-Class Group Analysis
- All students who are participating should read the same short story at the same time. (See marginal note.)

Group

- The worksheets ***Short Story Analysis*** (pg 18-9) contain the cards to use as guides for this activity.
- Have students work in small groups (I prefer three/group here.). There are six different cards, but more than one group can work on the same cards.
- Provide students with the short story and allow them time to read it to themselves.
- Give each group one Analysis card and allow them 10 min to discuss and answer the questions on their card.
- Have a member for each group read out the card then share their group's response with the class. Discuss.

Analyzing Science Fiction
Here is what students should gain by this activity
- **Awareness of the source**: The author is influenced by past experiences, culture, attitudes, and training, as well as by the message he or she wishes to convey through the story.
- **Awareness of the context**: A great story can be read and understood regardless of the time or setting. This being said, the social and political atmosphere when and where the story was written — the context — will have an impact. For example, I've found students better appreciate many stories written in the 1960's if they first learn about the Cold War.

Where to find it:
- Science fiction short stories are typically published in one of two formats, book anthologies (often around a theme) or in magazines. Of the magazines currently in print, *Asimov's* and *Analog* feature predominantly science fiction with a "hard" or fact-rooted premise. Collections of short stories which have won the Hugo and/or Nebula awards are published yearly as well. If students are choosing their own stories to read, just remind them it should be science fiction, not fantasy or horror.
- Information about authors, both science fiction and science, is most easily obtained through the Internet. There are also reference works such as "Works in Print" available at local libraries. Students could also contact authors or their publishers and request biographical information.

Stories from the Source
Science fiction authors are, in my experience, thrilled to know their work is being used by students. If you ask beforehand, many will grant you permission to copy one of their short stories for classroom use. Websites such as that of the Science Fiction and Fantasy Writers of America or the National Science Fiction Foundation (Canadian), list email addresses for member authors. Do not assume you have such permission until you have received a reply from the author.

a cure for cancer required the hearts of whales?

Where to find it:

- A selection of back issues of popular science magazines are usually available in science departments or libraries. The broader the range of types and quality you can show students, the better.

- You can obtain interesting responses by having some students critically read articles from textbooks, especially if you have some older examples available. While the science is typically passed through extensive review and edit, the underlying themes in science texts can vary from a application and technology focus to an environmental issue focus, to name only two notable swings in the education marketplace in the last decade.

Homework

Step II: Science Non-Fiction

Once you feel students have successfully applied critical reading skills to one or more science fiction stories, move immediately to the non-fiction part of this exercise. It's important to have students read non-fiction while they are still in the mind-set produced by the analysis of the story.

Choosing a science article to read

While you can have students read the same short story, I prefer to have as wide a variety of non-fiction examined by the class as possible. This is partly a time-saver, since you can undertake a comparison of credible and less-credible sources at the same time as honing critical reading with respect to individual articles and authors.

If you wish, have students bring in articles they find on their own. If they want to examine television reports, this can be done by requesting a transcript (usually at no or nominal cost) from the broadcasting station or, less effectively, by videotaping the segment. Regardless of source, students should have the article with them when you do this activity in the classroom.

Option A: Individual Analysis

- If class time is limited, and/or you feel confident your students gain proceed without further guidance, have them repeat this activity with a non-fiction science article, using the worksheet *Beyond Mere Words II* (pg 17), then discuss the entire exercise as a class. Focus on a comparison of the two research tasks.

- If you have more time, and/or you feel your students will need more help, take up the first portion of this activity as a class, making sure students are comfortable with the task, then have them analyze the non-fiction article on their own.

Option B - In-Class Group Analysis

- If you wish to have the class analyze one article together, then proceed as for the short story activity and simply substitute the article in place of the fiction, using the worksheet *Beyond Mere Words II* (pg 17). I recommend you do at least three non-fiction articles, with one being from a less credible source.

- If you wish to have each group analyze a different article, then discuss as a whole, I suggest giving each group *Analysis Cards # 3, 5,* and *6*. Focus the class discussion of each article on credibility of source and assumptions by the various authors about the scientific knowledge of readers.

What if...

Analyzing Science Non-Fiction

Here is what students should gain from this activity:

- **Awareness of the source**: It's not always possible to learn much about a non-fiction author, particularly those who report rarely in news media. The source, as a criterion for credibility, becomes the publication or venue used. Students should be able to list the clues they would use to help them rank such sources, including: any apparent bias revealed by other articles (including advertising, letters to the editor, etc.) in the same publication; reputation and/or history of the publication; process (Was the publication subject to peer review and editing? Internet sources frequently fail on this point.); and funding source.

- **Awareness of the context**: Unless you have students looking at older material, you are likely to be using non-fiction written within the students' own social and political atmosphere. This being the case, point to the publication itself as being an important indicator of context. (Hint: Have students check the Acknowledgments and/or funding sections.)

Extension Opportunities

Funny or Misleading?

Discover Magazine has, for the last few years, published "April Fool's" jokes in its "Breakthroughs" section of short articles. One memorable instance concerned the danger to Antarctic researchers of being attacked by giant mole rats, said rats being able to melt the ice beneath ones' feet with their hot heads. These articles are written in exactly the same style and tone as the others, although there are occasionally broad hints. (The name of the reporter for this article was "April Fool" in Italian, for example.)

Letters to the editor in subsequent issues usually contain one or more complaints about the latest joke, citing the hazard of presenting non-science alongside the credible work. Others are delighted by the chance to catch science in the act of being silly.

Have students debate this issue, assigning the roles of "reporter," "editor," and readers "for" and "against" the practice of these jokes. Be sure students consider the responsibility of the publication as a provider of information to non-scientists as well as the responsibility of non-scientist readers to be critical of what they read.

The Internet

As more and more people choose the Internet — with its astounding quantity of information — as their first choice when researching an issue or topic, it becomes even more vital to be critical of source and context. Carefully used, the Internet can be a superb means of finding valid, up-to-date answers. It is possible to contact many scientists directly about their work, allowing students unprecedented access to such expertise. Increasingly, one can even become a participant either through contribution or by using databases made available. This being said, there is also an access to misleading or inaccurate information as well. Be sure students are careful to question the source, use reputable websites, and look for confirmation of information from multiple sources. Establish the criteria acceptable in your classroom for Internet-based research, while encouraging students to learn how to use this resource.

it became possible to direct the movement of ocean currents?

Beyond Mere Words I

Story Title: _____

Author: _____

Publishing Information: _____

1. What is the scientific premise, the "what if..." underlying this story?
2. What is the attitude towards science portrayed in this story? Give an example.
3. How does the author present the scientific information needed as background to this story? (for example: an expert witness, narrative, assumption about readers' knowledge)
4. Where and when was this story first published (hint: check the copyright page and/or acknowledgments)?
5. What do you know about the author at this point?
6. What do you predict about the author based on this story?

Research: Find out as much as you can about the author and what was happening in the world at the time this story was first published.

Suggested Sources of Information About Authors

🗗 Public Libraries: carry or can access for you reference works with basic biographical information on published authors.

🗗 The Internet: Use a search engine and the author's name (you may have to experiment with using the full name or just the last name) or visit one of the major science fiction websites such as http://www.sff.net as a starting point.

🗗 The Author and/or Publisher: If time permits, contact the author (through the publisher if necessary) and ask your questions directly.

---

7. What have you learned about the author?
8. How does this compare with your predictions?
9. How do you think the author's views have been expressed in this story?
10. What influence, if any, do you think the original location and time of the publication of the story had on the view of science the author expressed? (Consider the social and political context as well as the state of science and/or technology.)
11. Think about your own views concerning the premise of this story. How would you change this story if it were yours? Why?

---

context: def'n. the circumstances relevant to something under consideration.

Article Title: _____

Author: _____

Publishing Information: _____

1. What is the scientific topic or issue being presented?

2. What is the attitude toward science presented in this article? Give an example. (Hint: is science the source of information and/or the source of some problem or controversy?)

3. (a) Where and when was this article first published (hint: check the copyright page and/or acknowledgments)?

   (b) In your opinion, does this make the scientific information in this article more or less credible? Explain your reasoning.

5. What do you know about the author at this point?

6. What do you predict about the author based on this article?

Research: Find out as much as you can about the author and what was happening in the world at the time this story was first published.

Suggested Sources of Information About Authors

⊡ Public Libraries: carry or can access for you reference works with basic biographical information on published authors.

⊡ The Internet: Use a search engine and the author's name (you may have to experiment with using the full name or just the last name). You may need to search under the name of the publication or the topic for previous articles by this author.

⊡ The Author and/or Publisher: If time permits, contact the author (through the publisher if necessary) and ask your questions directly.

---

7. How have your predictions about the author compared to what you have learned? What problems, if any, did you encounter finding information about the author?

8. How do you think the author's views have been expressed in the article?

9. How has learning more about the author affected your opinion about the credibility of this article?

10. What more would you like to know about the issue in this article? How would you find out?

credible: def'n. believable or worthy of belief; convincing.

Beyond Mere Words II

Story Analysis Cards

ANALYSIS CARD 1

Based on this story, how would you describe the author?
Think about:
• age
• sex
• physical description
• occupation (other than writing)
• education
• attitude towards science
• attitude towards people
• other

No Limits © Julie E. Czerneda & Trifolium Books Inc.

ANALYSIS CARD 2

What area of science is the author exploring in this story? How do you know?

• Biology
• Chemistry
• Physics
• Other

What is the scientific premise of this story? Express the main idea in a "what if" statement.

No Limits © Julie E. Czerneda & Trifolium Books Inc.

ANALYSIS CARD 3

<u>When</u> **do you think this story was written? What clues did you use to make this decision? What effect might this have had on the author's approach to this story's scientific premise?**

<u>Where</u> **do you think this story was written? What helped you decide? What effect might this have had on the author's approach to this story's scientific premise?**

No Limits © Julie E. Czerneda & Trifolium Books Inc.

ANALYSIS CARD 4

What point(s) is the author trying to make about science in this story?

Do you agree or disagree? Why?

No Limits © Julie E. Czerneda & Trifolium Books Inc.

ANALYSIS CARD 5

How did the author present the scientific information needed as background to this story?
• an expert witness (a character who knows and talks about the science)
• narrative (description)
• assumption (assumed a certain level of scientific knowledge from readers)

If there was an "expert witness," how did the author convince you that this character could be believed?

No Limits © Julie E. Czerneda & Trifolium Books Inc.

ANALYSIS CARD 6

What was the role of science presented in this story?
Think about:
• If any of the characters in the story were scientists, how were they portrayed?
• What role did science play in the problem that the characters faced in the story?
• What role did science play in the resolution of that problem?
• What does the author have to say about the significance of science to society (either today's or that portrayed in the story)?

No Limits © Julie E. Czerneda & Trifolium Books Inc.

Story Analysis Cards

Using Science Fiction to Investigate Popular Conceptions of Science and Scientists

Caution

Several teachers have told me that they use science fiction as an example to students of the flaws in popular conceptions about science and scientists. The problem with this is that science fiction literature often portrays science and scientists quite accurately and sympathetically. Students who try to use a novel or short story as a basis for a report on stereotypes can come away frustrated. Also, the negative approach of "let's find the flaws in the science" does less for students' understanding than "how could this work" or "which parts of this speculation are realistic and which parts are not?"

Scientific literacy is about effective and reliable communication of ideas, including being able to discern the meaningful from the misleading. If there is any aspect of science in which most students come to class with potentially misleading notions, it is in their understanding of science and those who call it their profession.

These notions are not solely the fault of portrayals in the various media. They also result from a lack of exposure to real people working in science other than the teacher or doctor. Few students have the opportunity to meet firsthand those who could help them perceive the type of interactions so central to scientific endeavor.

Science fiction can be used in a number of ways to help students better understand the difference between popular conceptions of science and scientists and the reality. Once they do, it is easier for them to understand how such conceptions can affect how they perceive and evaluation scientific information.

Science fiction can help:

1. To expose students' own stereotypical ideas;
2. In considering how science and scientists are portrayed in visual media and popular culture;
3. In considering how science and scientists are portrayed in science fiction literature.

You may wonder why I've distinguished between visual media and literature. By and large, science fiction literature shows science as helpful or essential to society, rather than as the source of a problem, and the role of the scientist is often either as expert witness or protagonist — not villain. This is true even if the "what if..." premise deals with some discovery or technology gone awry. In sharp contrast, much of television and film science fiction employs an irresponsible or "mad" scientist as frequent plot device and the science is something unleashed on an unsuspecting world. The scientist as hero is a relatively new phenomenon. There are exceptions, but a survey of the science fiction literature generally available in school libraries and films generally available for home rental will show this trend quite distinctly.

This means that science fiction literature can be a painless way to introduce students to science and scientists.

How to Proceed

Exposing Stereotypes and Preconceptions

You may have to trick your class into revealing their preconceptions and stereotypes — especially the older students who may honestly (and vehemently) feel themselves free of such things. One approach I've used successfully is to wait until the class is enthusiastically engaged in a story-plotting activity such as described on page 6. I have the students develop the characteristics of a protagonist (or expert witness) who will, in their story, "know or do the science." On a "show of hands" basis, similar to that used in the story-plotting activity, they build this character as I record the various features on the board.

Hint: In order to have this work, push the class through the character development as quickly as you can. Fire questions at them such as "Sex? Hands up for female. Hands up for male. Age? Hands up for over 20...etc."

Even the most liberal-minded, bright group of students I've had produced basically the following result if they've been unconscious of what was happening:

The scientist is:

- ☐ male
- ☐ white (*variations*: American, British)
- ☐ older (*variations*: ancient, elderly, over 40)
- ☐ wears glasses (*variations*: bad dresser, uncool)
- ☐ has no friends (*variations*: has no life, has no family)
- ☐ works alone (*variation*: anti-social, hates people)
- ☐ takes no responsibility for his work
- ☐ motivated by curiosity
- ☐ independently wealthy

All I've had to do is stand to one side, indicate the list of characteristics, and ask: "is this a typical scientist?" The usual reaction is an abashed silence. We then take a few moments to toss around ideas of what a "real" scientist might be like. I like to finish with a discussion of the science workplace and the fact that scientists very rarely work in isolation. Any examples you can bring to the discussion will be helpful.

Where to find it:
If you do not have copies of the student anthology, look for other science fiction stories with realistic scientists and science. Consult the list of recommended works on page 122.

Being Tactful
At some point in story-plotting, investigating preconceptions, or other activities, one or more students will reveal attitudes or ideas that could provoke ridicule from their peers. It's important to encourage the free expression of all ideas by making sure you are tactful when this occurs. I've found it helps if I can expose preconceptions and stereotypes of the group rather than of individuals. Then, you can take the sting out of the revelation by immediately turning attention to where such ideas come from, for example, the visual media.

Invite a scientist into the classroom to talk about various aspects of this career. If possible, take students to visit scientists at work, such as a food science laboratory or local research facility.

Mad or Nerd?
By modern standards, the classic mad scientist, particularly if a protagonist and not a villain, is a "brilliant nerd." This stereotype is just as offensive to real scientists as any other. But public perceptions are changing. See page 70 for activities to explore scientists as portrayed by "Other Media."

The movie *Contact*, winner of the 1998 Hugo Award for best dramatic presentation of SF, is also regarded by many scientists as finally showing the realities of their work. You may wish to arrange a viewing of this film as part of this lesson.

The Strength of Many

Stress with students that while individual scientists are "only human," the strength of science is in the insistence that acceptable results and conclusions are those which can be repeated by anyone else using the same procedure. This has particular significance in terms of developing of scientific literacy. Students should understand the risk of using only one source of information on a topic, or, as citizens, the risk of making decisions based on only one set of results or one set of conclusions about a scientific issue.

Where to find it:
Robert J. Sawyer's novels reflect his understanding and respect for practicing scientists and are highly recommended. Have students read the acknowledgment section of his books.

From the Horse's Mouth

While most science fiction writers are not scientists, there are notable exceptions, including:
- Isaac Asimov, physicist
- Gregory Benford, physicist
- David Brin, physicist
- Geoff Landis, software designer (Mars missions)
- Joan Slonczewski, molecular biologist

The Mad Scientist Mythology

- Use the worksheet, *Recipe: A Mad Scientist* (pg 24), to generate ideas of how scientists are portrayed in visual and news media (again, I make a distinction with science fiction literature here).
- Once you have the stereotypes identified, have students read a science fiction story such as "Stream of Consciousness" by Robert J. Sawyer from the companion anthology *Packing Fraction and Other Tales of Science & Imagination*. They should complete the worksheet, *The Real Thing* (pg 25), using the protagonist of the story as a model.

The Real Thing

Here is what students should gain from these activities:
An appreciation that science is:
- most often a team or group effort;
- conducted (and/or supported) by businesses and industries, organizations, institutions, and governments;
- an activity that relies heavily on the contributions of others, past and present;
- undertaken to solve problems (including design or technology problems such as commercial applications), expand understanding, and predict consequences.

An appreciation that scientists:
- are a diverse group of human beings;
- are affected by their own beliefs and convictions, as well as the context of their society and culture. This being said, scientists rely on the scientific method and peer review to maintain the essential reproducibility and reliability their work demands;
- may spend a significant portion of their time in administration and other duties related to funding their work and/ or managing others;
- may be motivated, as any set of human beings, by varying degrees of altruism and / or self-interest.

Other Approaches

Instead of using the story-plotting activity, you can simply ask students to describe a scientist and proceed to generate a list of characteristics as a class. You are more likely to get the answers the class judges to be "correct" than to reveal as much to the students themselves. However, if you then use the worksheet *Recipe: A Mad Scientist* (pg 24), you can help students identify stereotypes and preconceptions from popular media.

What if...

Extension Opportunities

Post-secondary Statistics
Have students visit the guidance department (or use the Internet) to obtain statistics on who is graduating with science degrees. They can investigate gender roles, the pattern of change over the last two decades in various fields, career prospects, etc.

Community Survey
Students design and conduct a survey to find out whose quoted opinion about a science-based issue would matter most to members of their community, that of: a scientist, a government official, a member of a non-profit group, a teacher, a doctor, an activist, a local businessperson or an elected politician. Have them draw conclusions about the decision-making process.

Science Fiction Conventions
SF conventions consist of panels in which guests discuss specific topics and answer audience questions, as well as film screenings, masquerades, art shows, and dealers. I've taken students to conventions for the past ten years and have nothing but praise for the experience. The people attending conventions are interested in science, imaginative, and willingly converse with students. Panels range within three broad categories: science (at my last convention, this included astronomy, paleontology, cybernetics, and the human genome project: all by scientists working in those fields), the creative crafts (writing, illustrating, screenwork, acting etc.), and science fiction itself in all its forms. Many conventions provide fantasy, horror, and gaming panels as well. There is a growing trend to include panels for educators, ranging from young adult literature to science fiction in the classroom. The 1998 Worldcon in Baltimore featured a day of programming linked to schools, including a non-fiction and fiction writing contest for students.

Interviewing a Scientist
- If possible, have students interview a scientist. They can use the worksheet, **The Real Thing** (pg 25) as a guide to developing their own questions. (Hint: you might also want to provide **The Business of Science**, pg 40, as well.) As a further link to scientific literacy, invite the scientist to provide sample publications you can compare with popular science materials.
- Arrange a tour of a local laboratory or other scientific establishment in your community for students (or invite a student who has completed a co-op placement in such an establishment to the class).

Website

See page 118 for recommended websites.

Where to find it:
Students planning a survey could use the worksheet, *I Want to Believe! Survey* (page 59), as a model.

Convention Tips
If you've never attended a science fiction convention before, here are some tips:
- dress casually: panelists such as guest authors may wear office-type clothing, but most in attendance prefer interesting T-shirts and casual pants. (5-10 % of fans wear costumes, particularly at Star Trek conventions);
- if you can't attend the full weekend, Saturday usually offers the most in terms of panels;
- if you have special needs or requirements, let the convention staff know. All science fiction conventions pride themselves on being full-access;
- don't be deceived by appearances. The average attendee is a well-educated professional, no matter what he or she is wearing;
- take business cards so you can quickly exchange email or other contact information with individuals you wish to reach after the convention. The majority of convention guests are very approachable and willing to help.

---

faster-than-light travel was possible, just for babies?

Recipe: A Mad Scientist

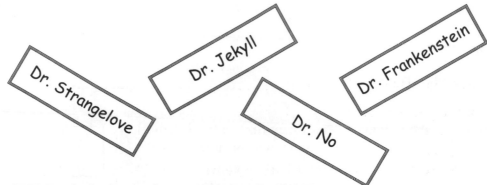

Dr. Strangelove

Dr. Jekyll

Dr. No

Dr. Frankenstein

Watch the beginnings of science fiction films from the 60's onward and there's no doubt about it: in most cases, science is the bad guy. And who is that turns science into a loaded gun aimed at the rest of humanity?

The Mad Scientist!

How do we recognize this classic character? Filmmakers might almost be using a recipe when it comes to showing us a scientist. What are the main ingredients?

Based on your own experience or by watching some science fiction films (yes, that would be homework), record the ingredients for a mad scientist.

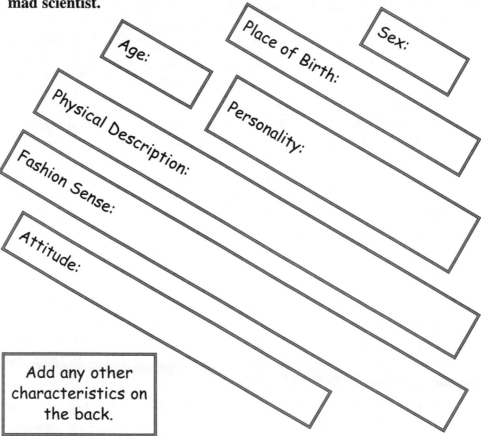

Age:

Place of Birth:

Sex:

Physical Description:

Personality:

Fashion Sense:

Attitude:

Add any other characteristics on the back.

mad: def'n. insane; having a disordered mind; wildly foolish; wildly excited or infatuated; angry; rabid; wildly light-hearted.

Name of Scientist Profiled: _____

If this is a science fictional character:
Title of Story:
Author:
Context (setting and time of publication):

If this is an actual person:
How did you find this scientist?
Where does this scientist work?
In which field(s) of science does this scientist work?

You may or may not find all of the answers to the remaining questions. For any you cannot answer, think of how you could obtain this information.

1. How much education is required for this work?

2. Who or what supplies financial support for the work of this scientist?

3. What is a typical work day for this scientist? (Include other people he or she interacts with, as well as tasks and equipment.)

4. What does the scientist think about this work? (For example, is this area of science personally important, important to society, or "just a job?") How do you know?

5. (a) Does this scientist need to communicate information about his or her work to non-scientists? If so, describe how this communication usually takes place.

   (b) Does this scientist ever experience frustration or difficulty in communicating with non-scientist? If so, what is the cause?

6. Based on your opinion of this scientist, predict how he or she might react in each of the following situations:

   (a) The scientist is incorrectly quoted in a newspaper article.

   (b) The scientist's name is incorrectly linked with an environmental problem.

   (c) Some aspect of the scientist's research is used for criminal or dangerous purposes.

7. How important is peer review to the work of this scientist? (Peer review is the process in which other scientists attempt to reproduce the results of the first in order to check their credibility.)

peer: def'n. a person who is equal in ability, standing, rank, or value: a contemporary.

The Real Thing

Where to find it:
- Information about contests can be obtained from local libraries, writers' groups and associations, museums, and government agencies. The Internet is the best source, since up-to-date submission requirements are usually posted and can be bookmarked or printed for interested students.
- Mentors can be older students (including alumni), local writers and editors, or staff members. While a mentor can be extremely helpful for young writers, it is important to ensure the mentor is familiar with the style or genre of writing the student wishes to explore.

Website

See page 118 for sites of interest to new writers.

Special Note: Encouraging Students Beyond the Classroom

Writing Fiction

You may find, as I have, that introducing science fiction into the classroom reveals the latent writers, those too shy to speak out before. I've also found keeping those students writing to be like starting a fire in damp wood with a handful of nice dry tinder. Wonderful flame and sparks to begin with, then smoke, then hardly a glow unless you work at it. Fortunately, it doesn't take a great deal in terms of resources or time to fan the flames of creativity. Here are some suggestions:

- Arranging mentors. A critical and compassionate mentor can be incredibly helpful to a young writer. A poor mentor may be worse than none at all. If you arrange mentorships, start with a trial period and allow both parties an easy escape in case the pairing isn't working.
- Offer time and space to a school writers' group. These do best when very structured and each member provides new work to be critiqued by the others at every meeting. There are websites with information on setting up and running writers' groups.

Group

- Work with the language arts department and library staff to invite writers to conduct workshops for interested students.
- Set up a bulletin board or webpage with resources on careers in writing, marketplaces for work, contests, etc. Most writers begin their careers while in school or working elsewhere.

Scientific Literacy

You can continue to promote the goals of scientific literacy outside of the classroom in several ways. Here are just a few:

- Science clubs. It isn't easy to start or maintain a school science club, yet it can be an excellent venue to encourage scientific literacy among involved students. Try linking your club to one at a university, either on-line or by monthly visits if possible. Arrange for club members to participate in national or international data-gathering exercises.
- Recognizing excellence in science writing. For example, host a local issue science background contest with winners to be published in the community newspaper.

What if...

Speculating about Issues in Physics

"...At the sub-atomic level we have much more exciting possibilities..."

from *Packing Fraction*
by Charles Sheffield

If you look carefully at this illustration, you will see how Larry Stewart took into account the various representations of an atom a student might encounter, depending on the age of the resources they are using at the time. By including both the older orbital style and the newer shell model, he hoped to make his atoms immediately clear regardless of the reader's experience.

Packing Fraction

by Charles Sheffield

Midnight: when churchyards yawn, and graves give up their dead.

In my department, of course, the action begins a bit later; say, about one o'clock, when some drivers on the road ought not to be, when the bars have emptied and the few who don't want to go home turn nasty, and when incidents of domestic violence progress beyond the shouting stage. Tonight none of that applied. We were dead-dog quiet, as though the event of three days ago had bled all other violence from the world. And at the same time we were on full twenty-four hour alert, because if such a disaster could strike only thirty miles away, with no warning and no reason, why couldn't it happen here?

It was close to 2:30, and I was idly watching the monitors with their cross-country news feeds when Hambley called from the front desk downstairs.

"Sir? It might be a good idea for you to come down."

"A loud one?"

"No. Very quiet. But I think you ought to hear him." There was a moment's hesitation, then Hambley added in a lower voice, "He says he has an idea what happened in Frederick."

That was enough. I started down, but not before I had activated the tie-line. It normally went to County Headquarters, but for the past three days it also went downtown to Washington, to the FBI, ATF, State Department, CIA, and god-knows how many other government agencies that nobody was going to tell me about.

The man sitting at the desk across from Officer Hambley didn't look like a threat to anyone. If he were part of the unknown terrorist group which had blown Frederick off the map, he was the most unlikely candidate I had ever seen. He wore a charcoal-gray business suit with a white shirt and a tie of subdued blue check, and even in the pre-dawn hours of stubble and dark despair he was newly shaven. Only his eyes told a different story. He glanced up for a moment as I approached, and the pale-blue irises were surrounded by bloodshot whites and their black surrounds. Raccoon eyes. They suggested that in the past three days he had managed even less sleep than me.

Reading Level
Most high school students. You may wish to provide a list of the more specialized terms used in this story to assist ESL and other less experienced readers.

What if...
The author was asked to base his story on some aspect of physics. He chose to speculate on what might happen if a person were able to push atoms closer together than they naturally exist, hence altering their packing fraction - how many atoms can be in a prescribed volume. It is a harmless-sounding "what if...." and the author describes several practical applications. But there is a problem.

"...activated the tie-line..." This is a crucial plot point. The author emphasizes throughout this story that it is not one man listening to another in confidence. All that is said is being carried far beyond the room.

Hambley had provided coffee. The man sat with the cup clenched in both hands. I went to the seat next to him.

"I'm Captain Corrigan." I did not offer my hand. "I understand that you think you may have a line to the people who blew up Frederick."

He nodded, and I began to make the usual statement protecting his rights. If he had been directly involved he was going to need it. More than thirty thousand people had died in Frederick on Monday evening, and the final count was still not in. He waved my warning aside.

"I think I know who did it, and I have an idea how it happened. But I had no part of it." He was being recorded, voice and picture. By this time I suspected that a hundred people were watching him on live feeds. It wasn't even necessary to prompt him. The words came spilling out as though he had been rehearsing them for three days.

"My name is Alan Parseghian. I am the president of a small company, YCA Research, here in Rockville."

I gave a nod to Officer Hambley, who turned to his terminal. He would check out the name, together with the company, and a car would be over there in less than five minutes. Speed might be important — no matter what Parseghian might think.

"I live near the office," he went on. "Walking distance. I'm single, and I tend to work late. It was just after seven o'clock, eight days ago, when I had a visitor. It was a woman, and I didn't remember meeting her before.

"You might think that sounds peculiar, somebody arriving unannounced at my office after working hours. But it's not. For one thing, when I'm really busy I don't usually answer the phone after five. My answering machine tells a caller whether or not I'm still there. Also, when you're a small business you get used to the idea of sharing resources to reduce costs. The best time to have access to somebody else's equipment is second or third shift, when they're done with it for the day. I'd say that someone comes around to ask if they can rent time on my fabrication line, maybe three or four times a month."

Alan Parseghian showed no sign of needing to be prompted, but there was one question I had to ask.

"Your company, Mr. Parseghian. Does it have anything to do with nuclear materials?"

He shook his head. The question did not seem to surprise him. Unless he was totally cut off from the world he would

Many students are unfamiliar with the concept of science as a "business." The description of Parseghian's small hi-tech firm and how it operates is quite true to life, being somewhat based on the author's own lifestyle. You may want to emphasize with students that a great deal of scientific research, particularly into applications, is conducted by smaller, focussed businesses such as this one. Interested students could verify this for themselves by generating a list of some of the suppliers to NASA.

know that the town of Frederick had been annihilated by a nuclear device, with an estimated yield of one hundred kilotons. That's bigger than was used on Hiroshima or Nagasaki, and Frederick is — was — a small town. A bomb of that size was total overkill. One major speculation was that the terrorists had been planning to hit Washington DC, and had somehow triggered the fusion reaction before they could ship it downtown.

"We're high-tech," he went on. "But not nuclear. Space is our business. We make propellant storage vessels for small-sats, and recently we've been moving into the big tanks used for main launch propellant storage. Liquid oxygen, liquid hydrogen — like they use with the Shuttle External Tank. Big, big volumes of material, low density and awkward to haul around."

He must have seen my eyes beginning to glaze over, because he added, "This is all relevant, Captain Corrigan." Exhausted or not, he had remembered my name after one hearing. "We had just received a NASA Request for Proposal for a lighter and stronger bulk storage tank. Janice Jarnile — that's the name she gave me — said she'd heard through the grapevine that we were probably going to bid, but she thought we didn't have much of a chance.

"Spelling?"

Instead of answering my question in words, he silently fished a business card from his top pocket and handed it to me. It read: Janice Jarnile, Ph.D. Chief Scientist, Industrial Solutions, Inc. And then, the part that really grabbed my attention: 340 Hood Road, Frederick, MD.

"It is, Captain Corrigan." He had seen my eyes turning to the new big wall map, which showed the town of Frederick and the zones for different levels of devastation. "Hood Road is not merely within the area of destruction, it is at the center of it. The offices of Industrial Solutions no longer exist.

"According to Janice Jarnile, they were never very extensive. She was quite frank with me that first evening — or seemed to be. She admitted that she was pretty much a one-woman operation, a research chemist with DuPont up in Delaware until she decided she would rather work for herself. Her specialty was industrial solvents — Industrial Solutions, you see, quite a neat name for her company. But nothing, as I told her after ten minutes of general conversation, to do with my line of work. Had she, perhaps, been misled as to YCA's business specialty?

There are several abbreviations and unusual terms used in this story. Encourage students to find the meanings of these on their own. When you go over these terms as a class, elicit the idea that using "jargon" may be helpful to those that "know" but can keep others from fully understanding what is said. If time permits, follow with an examination of jargon used in articles in popular science and other media.

Possibly new terms for students:
sat - satellite
propellant - fuel (hydrogen is the fuel, oxygen required for its use)
bid - as used here: an offer to do specific work for a certain price

No Limits   31

Jarnile's demonstration is one students can readily repeat for themselves. In fact, you may already be planning to do this or a similar demonstration of the space between atoms as part of your program on particle theory.

"She shook her head. She was a big, solidly-built redhead — I know, I am using the past tense — with a sort of smug look to her. Instead of answering my question, she asked, 'Got any coffee? — hot, for preference.'

"I assumed that she wanted to drink it, so I pointed to the pot and said, 'It's hot, but it's pretty well stewed. I'll make some more.'

"'No need,' she said. And she went across, helped herself to a clean cup from the rack, and filled it near to the brim with coffee. She reached over and picked up one of the dispensers.

"'Not that one!' I said. 'That's salt. Sugar is the one next to it.'

"'I know,' she said. She carried the full cup and the salt cellar back to where I was sitting. 'Now watch.'

"She took a spoon, filled it with salt, dumped it into the coffee, and stirred. While I watched, she did it again, over and over.

"'See?' she said.

"All I saw was that she had made herself a pretty undrinkable cup of coffee. I said as much, and she laughed. 'That's not the object of the exercise. The important thing is, when I brought this cup over here, it was almost full. I added a dozen or more spoons of salt — and the cup didn't spill over. Here's my question: Where did the salt go? Why isn't the volume of coffee plus salt — or water plus salt, it would work just as well with hot water — equal to the volume of the water, plus the volume of the salt?"

Alan Parseghian paused and looked at me. "Did I mention that I am a physicist by training, Captain Corrigan? Well, I am, but I have some knowledge of chemistry. Not as much as a real chemist, and certainly not as much as Janice Jarnile, but enough to try to answer her question."

"'When the salt dissolves in water it dissociates,' I said. 'It is sodium chloride, so it breaks up to form sodium and chlorine ions. The ions can sort of fit into the spaces between the water molecules, so the water/salt combination occupies less space than the sum of the two original volumes. You get the same sort of thing when you mix water and alcohol.'

"'Precisely.' She spoke as though I was an unusually apt fifth-grader, which I didn't much care for; but I didn't have time to say so, because she at once reached into her pocket and took out a cylindrical flask, about the size of a fat bottle of pills.

"'This is a Dewar,' she said. 'Designed for low-temperature storage of materials. I'm assuming, given your business, that you keep a supply of liquid hydrogen and liquid oxygen here on the premises.'

"'Not a lot,' I said. 'This is our R&D shop. But I have more than enough to fill something that small. Which do you want?'

"'Make it liquid hydrogen. And arrange a way to transfer it to this flask.'

"'How much?' I squinted at the little bottle. 'About fifty c.c.'s?'

"'Don't worry about that. Bring plenty — several liters. Can you meter the transfer?'

"It seemed easier to humor her than to argue. I handle LH and LOX — liquid hydrogen and liquid oxygen — all the time, so we have built-in safety procedures. I transferred a few liters to one of our own big Dewars, and watched the fog form in the air — liquid hydrogen boils at two hundred and fifty degrees below freezing. I arranged for a slow metered feed, thermally shielded, into the little bottle that Janice Jarnile had brought with her.

"'What you said about salt and water sharing space is quite accurate.' She was not even watching the flowmeter. 'But that's at the molecular level. At the sub-atomic level we have much more exciting possibilities. Do you realize that an atom is almost all space?'

"It was another patronizing question — and in my own field, physics.'

"'Of course I do,' I said. 'The nucleus is just a couple of fermis across, while the whole atom is a nanometer or so. Only one part in a trillion is matter, the rest is empty space.

"'So inefficient,' she said. 'A packing fraction of one in a trillion. If you could increase that to even one in a billion, think how much it would change the economics of storing light substances — like liquid hydrogen. Think how small you could make a propellant tank.'

"I was thinking of exactly that, and the upcoming NASA proposal. Anyone who could offer a tank one-tenth the size of the other proposers, with the capacity to carry as much fuel as anyone else, would be a shoo-in. But I was also aware that what Janice Jarnile was saying was quite impossible. Atoms can't move closer together, no matter how useful that would be. They are held strongly apart because their electron shells repel each other electrically.

Dewars - container for low temperature storage (i.e. sophisticated thermos bottle)
R&D - research and development
LH - liquid hydrogen
LOX - liquid oxygen

You could ask students for analogies at this point. One I particularly liked was to be able to put the contents of a full backpack into one small pocket. Sounded convenient, until they realized the pocketful would be so heavy it might rip from the coat.

"I said as much to my visitor, but at the same time I had my eye on the flowmeter. It insisted that two and a half liters of liquid hydrogen had been transferred to the tiny flask that Janice Jarnile had brought with her. Unless I refused to believe my own eyes and instruments, an impossible packing density of matter was being achieved, even as I watched, in the flask in front of me.

"'Of course it's not easy.' She smirked at me. 'Otherwise, they'd all be doing it. There is a special trick, a field inside the Dewar. It's what I call a Jarnile Field, and it adjusts the phase of the quantum state vectors. Electromagnetically speaking, the atoms inside the flask aren't aware of each other. They can move much closer together, because they don't feel the electrostatic repulsion.'

"'What happens if you turn off the field?' I had decided in the past two minutes that although I didn't like Janice Jarnile, she had ten times my brains — and as my friends will tell you, Captain Corrigan, I am not generally known as a modest man.'

"'I wouldn't recommend it,' she said. 'The electrostatic repulsion between the atoms of hydrogen would return to normal, and either the flask would explode or liquid hydrogen would come out of the top as a high-pressure jet. Don't worry, we'll build in all sorts of safeguards for the NASA proposal. Assuming you are interested, that is. If not, there are plenty of others who will be. The Jarnile Field has a thousand different applications, yours is just one of the first and easiest.' She turned off the flow, removed the delivery tube, and put the cap on her little flask. Without speaking she picked it up and handed it to me. It weighed at least a kilo. The flowmeter insisted that more than seven liters of liquid hydrogen had been transferred to the flask's tiny interior.

Suggest "...a thousand different applications..." as a starting point for student stories based on the "what if." premise of this story.

"'And this is nowhere near the limit,' she said. 'I'm working on the design of a Jarnile Field that should improve the packing fraction by another four orders of magnitude. I will call you on Tuesday morning, Mr. Parseghian, and we can talk terms. I'll tell you now, I expect adequate compensation. Without me I don't think you have a prayer for the NASA procurement — and if this works out I can point your company toward a hundred other business opportunities.'

"She left. She didn't call on Tuesday, but of course by that time I wasn't expecting it. If she had been in Frederick when the bomb went off, she was reduced to dust, and her discovery would have died with her.

"Then on Tuesday afternoon my brain started to work. Janice Jarnile comes to see me from Frederick on Thursday evening, with a revolutionary new idea. She says she will call me on Tuesday morning to talk terms. On Monday, the whole town of Frederick is wiped off the face of the earth, including Janice Jarnile and her invention. An unfortunate accident of timing? Coincidences certainly happen. But maybe this wasn't one. Not considering what the Jarnile Field does."

Parseghian paused, as though he had just told me something highly significant.

Maybe he had. Or maybe he was exhausted past the point of being rational. I've seen that happen often enough.

"I don't see what you are getting at," I said at last. "This"— I glanced again at her business card — "this Dr. Jarnile had a way of packing a whole lot of stuff into a very small space. OK, that sounds clever and pretty useful. But we're dealing in Frederick with a major disaster, a terrorist bomb that took a whole Maryland town off the map. She worked in Frederick, but so what? Those two things have nothing to do with each other. What's your point?"

Parseghian stared directly at me, with those worried raccoon eyes. Instead of answering my question, he seemed to go off in another direction completely. "There has been non-stop news coverage of the explosion, but not many technical details. It was nuclear, and the radioactive by-products indicate that it was nuclear fusion, not nuclear fission. More like an H-bomb than the old-fashioned A-bomb that ended the Second World War. But peculiar radiation products, the experts say, even for a small H-bomb. More like some new kind of fusion weapon that no one has ever seen before."

"So?" I was beginning to think that I sounded stupid, and I don't like that, especially with who-knew-how-many others listening on the other ends of the live feed. It's my job to hear lots of facts and make connections quickly. Maybe I was exhausted too, because Parseghian seemed to me to be just rambling. And now off he went in another direction.

"I started thinking. I thought about Janice Jarnile, and the fact that she claimed to be a chemist rather than a physicist. The Jarnile Field allowed atoms to ignore each other's electrostatic repulsion, so they could get closer together. That means you could pack more of them into the same space. But when you do that, the nuclei of the atoms get closer together. If you get them close enough, there is a chance of something new happening: spontaneous fusion, in which the nuclei of a material — say,

Note the reminder that others are listening.

A very important point is made here concerning specialization in science. The statement "...she claimed to be a chemist rather than a physicist..." implies that Jarnile lacked knowledge or training which would have warned her of the risks. Discuss with students the advantages and disadvantages of having panels of experts from different fields assess new technologies or discoveries.

There is an interesting process going on here, as the investigator becomes convinced it was an accident rather than a terrorist attack - supposedly meaning it is unlikely to happen again. The reader shares the character's relief. But when he asks for further reassurance, "...Nobody else is likely to stumble onto the same thing..." Parseghian reveals how easy it would be to repeat Jarnile's work: so easy he hesitated to come forward with the truth at first, in case someone "...used the knowledge in the wrong way..."

hydrogen — combine to form another material — say, helium. That's the reaction that keeps the sun shining. Do it on a smaller scale, and you have a fusion bomb.

"When Janice Jarnile left on Thursday night, she told me she was working to increase the packing fraction by several orders of magnitude. She would try to push the nuclei in the little flask closer and closer together. On Monday afternoon, I think she succeeded in a way that she had never expected."

Alan Parseghian leaned back and closed his eyes. I stared at the camera, still recording. I hadn't understood all of what he had told me, but I finally had enough to draw my own conclusions.

"You're telling me, it's not terrorists," I said slowly. "Nobody wanted to blow up Frederick. No one was planning to take out Washington, or New York, or Philly."

"That is what I believe. Janice Jarnile wanted money, and maybe later, fame. What happened in Frederick was pure accident."

"And she was a real genius, you think. Nobody else is likely to stumble onto the same thing."

The pale-blue eyes popped open and he frowned at me. "Did I say that? If so, I did not mean to. Once a scientist has shown that something can be done, a much lesser scientist can follow. Even I would have a good chance of creating the Jarnile Field, although this is not my field of expertise. But I can assure you of one thing, Captain Corrigan: I will not be the man who does so." He sighed, and closed his eyes again. "I wondered over and over if I ought to come and see you, or if I should try to withhold knowledge that might be used in the wrong way. However, I am glad that I came. Even if I am wrong, I feel I have acted responsibly. Others will take over now."

I glanced again at the camera, which had been feeding Alan Parseghian's words and images away to an undefined number of eyes and ears. Who were they, and what might their motives be?

"Very glad I came," Parseghian added drowsily. He sounded relieved, even relaxed. "I have not slept for days. I will sleep now."

My eyes turned to the wall map, where most of a square mile of the town of Frederick was marked as concentric rings of fused rubble and devastated buildings.

Janice Jarnile's invention had been made in a small lab, with limited resources. There must be thousands such, scattered all across the United States. I doubted if the location of all of them was known to any authority. And then there were the other labs, here and abroad, genuinely devoted to terrorism. All they needed was a lead, together with the assurance that it could be done.

I looked again at Alan Parseghian. He still sat in the uncomfortable metal-frame chair, but his eyes remained closed and he was breathing easily.

Just as he said, he could sleep now. I wondered how long it would be before I could.

The End

After reading and summarizing *Packing Fraction*, you may wish to hold a class debate on the pros and cons of this statement: "If a person allows an idea, such as a potentially dangerous technology, to be shared by other people, that person is responsible for any harm that might result."

Sheffield, Charles

(Note: this is not a complete list!)

My Brother's Keeper ACE Books 1982

The Selkie (with D. Bischoff) Macmillan 1982

The Web Between the Worlds Del Rey 1988

Trader's World Del Rey 1988

The Heritage Universe series Del Rey 1990-92

Cold as Ice TOR Books 1992

Brother to Dragons Baen Books 1992

The Mind Pool Baen Books 1993

Godspeed TOR Books 1993

The Judas Cross (with D. Bischoff) Warner Books 1994

Proteus in the Underworld Baen Books 1995

The Ganymede Club TOR Books 1995

Convergence: The Return of the Builders Baen Books 1997

Tomorrow and Tomorrow Bantam Books 1997

Putting Up Roots TOR Books 1997

Aftermath Bantam Books 1998

The Cyborg from Earth TOR Books (1998)

The Jupiter series (more to come):

Higher Education (with Jerry Pournelle) TOR Books 1996

The Billion Dollar Boy TOR Books 1997

Charles' short fiction can be found in numerous science fiction anthologies and magazines, including *Georgia on My Mind and Other Places*, a collection including his novelette *Georgia on my Mind* winner of the 1993 Hugo and Nebula awards.

Website

See page 118 for a site about Charles' work.

Meet Charles Sheffield

There's a bark from outside the glass doors and Charles Sheffield chuckles. "There's my main distraction. My Samoyed has never figured out that when I sit down to write I'm not about to take him for another walk."

"...relentless when interested..."

Charles describes himself as fundamentally lazy. "A good friend told me I was relentless when interested in something," he says. "I'd never thought of myself that way, but it's true. I'll go to extremes then."

Charles is a mathematician and a physicist. His particular interest — at the moment — is Astrophysics. "I'm Chief Scientist and Board Member of Earth Satellite Corporation," Charles explains. "I spend about half of my time working on scientific projects and the other half writing science fiction."

He didn't start writing until he needed it. "My first wife was terminally ill. It was a very difficult time," he recalls sadly. "When I think back, I realize that I started writing then at least in part because I needed an escape from reality — and also because it was something in my life I could control."

Charles has written over thirty novels since. His latest books pay tribute to the science fiction he enjoyed as a teen.

"...books to stretch their imaginations."

"I could pick from an incredible variety of writers. Today, there's so much media-based SF that it's hard for young readers to find books to stretch their imaginations." Charles created the *Jupiter* series to help fill that gap. "I'm excited by the prospect that my kids will be reading these books — and getting hooked!"

Charles' Top Three

"Three SF books with great science concepts, easy to find, and fun to read? That took some thought. Many classics have little science or are out-of-date. Many recent books, with better science, are hard to find in libraries. I know of good SF books that don't have much science at all.

"I recommend: *Mission of Gravity* by Hal Clement, *Wyrm* by Mark Fabi, and *Ender's Game*, by Orson Scott Card."

Lesson Suggestions

The author, Dr. Charles Sheffield, was born and educated in England. Among his many roles, he has served as a consultant to NASA Headquarters, an advisor to the Congressional Office of Technology Assessment, and as an expert witness to both House and Senate. He is Past-President and Fellow of the American Astronautical Society, a Fellow of the American Association for the Advancement of Science, Past-President of the Science Fiction Writers of America, and Member of the International Astronomical Union, among others. He continues to be very active in both science and science fiction, earning much-deserved respect and admiration in both fields.

Where to find it:
If you do not have copies of the student anthology, several of the activities here can be used with other science fiction stories. Consult the list of recommended works starting on page 120.

Lesson: Encouraging Creativity

Have students read this story, then work in groups to design a new technology other than fuel bottles that could employ the concept of "reduced packing fraction" to accomplish a task. They can present their technology:
- as a drawing with written explanation
- as described within a short story based on the technology and its potential risks and benefits
- as a model

Lesson: Critical Reading Skills

Use the profile of Charles Sheffield to help analyze the role of the author and cultural context in producing the particular interpretation of science that is presented in *Packing Fraction*. This story was written in July, 1996. Have students investigate what other events were taking place at this time in North America.

Lesson: Popular Views of Science and Scientists

- After reading this story, have students consider the business-side of science using the worksheet **The Business of Science** (pg 40) as a guide. The last question asks them to consider scenarios concerning a new business. See marginal note.
- To encourage students to think about the skills they acquire during science class, have them complete the worksheet *Science Skills Checklist* (pg 41) as though they were preparing for an interview at the business of the main character in the story or at any similar workplace.
- If possible, arrange for a visit by a scientist from the business community or a tour of a local business that relies on science.

The Business of Science

The scenarios given in the last question on this worksheet have no right or wrong answers. These are common situations faced by scientists moving into business. The most productive approach in the case of the employer claiming rights is to be sure to fully document private research — and to read your contract carefully. Some contracts include "own time" discoveries, but they may also provide support for turning these discoveries into businesses. (In fact, this is a growing trend, particularly in computer R&D firms.) In the second case, where another, competing business has already started, the person has the option of competing or finding their own unique niche or trying something else.

The last scenario, of being unable to communicate, is all too common. There are science writers who make a very good living translating proposals to bankers and other potential supporters. Be sure to emphasize the vital importance of good communication skills.

There are additional lesson ideas on page 42.

The Business of Science

1. List as many kinds of businesses as you can which are based on science (use another sheet of paper if necessary). Compare your list with that of other classmates until you have at least 10. One good place to look is the Yellow Pages of the phone book.

2. From your list, identify two businesses for each of these categories:

Research and Development (R&D)

_____   _____

Manufacturing

_____   _____

Service

_____   _____

A Combination of R& D and either Manufacturing or Service

_____   _____

3. What, if anything, do these "Research and Development" businesses have in common?

4. What, if anything, do the "Manufacturing" businesses have in common?

5. What, if anything, do the "Service" businesses have in common?

6. Based on your answers to the previous questions, is there a pattern to which types of science translate into various business ventures?

7. *Packing Fraction* by Charles Sheffield, features a scientist who is president of a company, YCA Research. In which of the categories from question #2 would you place this company? Why?

8. Return to your original list and sort all of the businesses into the categories from question #2. Which category contains the most businesses? Why do you think this is so? (Hint: are you considering only local businesses? If so, what factors might affect those?)

9. An important part of starting a new business is a business plan. A business plan is partly an educated guess at how an idea or product might sell over the next few years. Imagine you've made an amazing scientific discovery on your own time and believe it could become a successful business for you. What would you do if:
(a) You ask your boss to review your business plan, only to have your boss claim to own your idea.
(b) You find out someone else has already created a business based on an essentially similar idea.
(c) It's a great idea, but you can't seem to explain it to non-scientists.

The president of YCA Research, Alan Parseghian, has announced that his company has won a contract to produce bulk storage tanks for a new type of space craft and will be hiring a variety of skilled workers immediately, including student apprentices to work part-time in the laboratory and in quality control in the assembly plant.

You have some work experience, but nothing for a science-based company. Then you think about your high school science classes. What skills did you acquire that might help you get one of these jobs?

1. The following chart lists several science skills. For each one, put a checkmark in the column that you feel best describes your ability with that skill.
    None - You do not have this skill.
    Some - You understand what you are to do but prefer to follow instructions or diagrams.
    Very Skilled - You use this skill confidently, without supervision.

2. How can you move more of your skills into the "Very Skilled" category?

Science Skills Checklist

Skill	None	Some	Very Skilled
• communicating with others	☐	☐	☐
• designing and/or conducting an experiment to evaluate an hypothesis	☐	☐	☐
• distinguishing between conclusions, inferences, and recommendations	☐	☐	☐
• evaluating sources of error	☐	☐	☐
• graphing	☐	☐	☐
• identifying the components (variables, hypothesis, operational definitions, data collection) of a survey	☐	☐	☐
• identifying trends between variables from graphed data	☐	☐	☐
• identifying variables in a given event or relationship	☐	☐	☐
• interpreting data, including identifying appropriate and inappropriate interpretations	☐	☐	☐
• making logical inferences	☐	☐	☐
• making thoughtful observations	☐	☐	☐
• measuring mass & volume	☐	☐	☐
• measuring size & distance	☐	☐	☐
• stating testable hypotheses	☐	☐	☐
• working with others	☐	☐	☐
• writing reports	☐	☐	☐

If students complete the worksheet, *Science Skills Checklist* (pg 41), suggest they keep the completed (and dated) list with their other career search materials. They can update this list as they improve and/or add to their accomplishments in science.

See you in court.
Have students reenact a courtroom drama, using the information and characters presented in *Packing Fraction*, to determine the "facts" of the case. This reenactment could be shared with other classes who haven't read the story.

Additional Lesson Ideas - *Packing Fraction*

Lesson: The Particle Theory
Have students read this story as a followup to your activities concerning the particle theory, such as mixing equal volumes of water and alcohol. Emphasize the power of such a theory in suggesting further areas of research.

Lesson: Debate on Freedom of Information
After reading and discussing this story, hold a class debate on the pros and cons of a statement such as: "If a person allows an idea, such as a potentially dangerous technology, to be shared by other people, that person is responsible for any harm that might result." Guide the discussion into considerations of concepts such as:
* Who holds the responsibility for scientific or technological developments that may affect society? (The originator(s), the organization or institution financing the work, the government of the country in which the work takes place, etc.)
* What is the danger of barriers to the open exchange of ideas, particularly in science?

Lesson: Risk Analysis
Use this story as a starting point to a discussion of risk analysis, including:
* identification and assessment of risk;
* what constitutes acceptable versus unacceptable risk;
* safety standards and quality control in science.

Lesson: The Role of Peers in Science
There are two aspects which can be further investigated by students after reading this story: the idea of scientists working in groups, and the importance of peer review.
* While the scientists portrayed in this story are not shown as working in a team or group setting, science as a whole is presented as a network of individuals, laboratories, and facilities connected by information. Have students investigate how scientists work together at a distance and in groups, using examples from this story as well as outside resources.
* Discuss how peer review might have prevented the accident in the story. Have students perform an experiment in which peer review of their findings is an important step.

Speculating about Issues in Chemistry

"...We're really nothing more than just walking chemical factories..."

from *Love is Chemistry*
by Jan Stirling

For this illustration, Larry Stewart wanted to contrast the mysterious nature of love as people view it with the chemical concepts postulated in the story. There is a hidden image in the art you can challenge students to find. (Hint, the smoke is not all it seems to be.) Students who are interested in illustrating should note the importance of being able to draw everyday objects. The bottle here forms a key part of the overall image.

Love is Chemistry

by Jan Stirling

Crystal stabbed her fork into a leaf of lettuce in irritation. "Uncle Paul, that's an awful thing to say!"

"Well, I mean it," he answered, smiling indulgently at his niece. "What is traditionally thought of as romantic love is just chemistry."

Crystal shook her head in disbelief. *Probably never had a girlfriend*, she thought.

"I've always liked to think there was more to love than just chemistry," her mother said taking a sip of water. "Though that's part of it," she conceded.

"It's all of it," Paul insisted, looking smug. "Every move you make, every perception, every feeling you have is, in essence, a complex chemical reaction. We're really nothing more than just walking chemical factories. Which is why by next year I might be a millionaire."

Crystal's father raised his brows and Uncle Paul, the younger of the two brothers, hastened to explain.

"I've just about perfected an artificial pheromone that will get you more love than you can handle," he said proudly.

"Well, who wants more love than they can handle," Mom asked with a laugh.

"Therein lies its flaw," Uncle Paul said sadly.

"So, what's a pheromone?" Crystal asked.

"It's a class of hormonal substances, secreted by the skin in humans, that stimulates a behavioral response in other organisms of the same species."

Crystal looked at him askance. "So, what's a pheromone?" she repeated.

Paul rolled his eyes and said, "Remember that gypsy moth trap your dad put up? He got the stuff on his fingers and the moths were fluttering all around him. That was a trap that used pheromones as bait. Think of it as a very attractive scent. Those moths were in love with your father."

"Well I can't fault their taste," Mom said, smiling at Dad. He blew her a kiss.

God, Crystal thought, embarrassed, *I wish they wouldn't do that!* They'd been married forever, you'd think they'd have gotten

Reading Level
Accessible to most high school students. One of the strengths of this particular story is the author's sensitivity to the needs and feelings of teenagers. This is a good choice for those students who have never read science fiction and/or who are certain they wouldn't enjoy this genre.

What if...
For this story, the author was asked to explore some aspect of chemistry. Because of her interest in human interactions, she chose to investigate the possibilities and consequences of synthesizing a substance to influence how people relate to one another — a scientific love potion. As the mode of delivery is simple diffusion, this author was also able to have her characters deal with the ethical issues of testing such a substance.

Possibly new terms for students:
pheromone - a chemical substance secreted and released by an animal for detection and response by another of the same species.

hormone - a substance that stimulates cells or tissues into action; produced in an organism (many have been synthesized) and transported via body fluids such as blood.

secreted - in this instance, released by living cells.

species - organisms similar enough to breed and produce fertile offspring.

The author reveals a great deal about the character Paul when he describes the delivery method: a perfume. This implies the substance will be sold as a cosmetic in stores, even though it has a drug-like effect. This is a good example to use with students when discussing how to *show* rather than *tell* a plot point or other story element.

vomeronasal organ - (sometimes referred to as Jacobson's Organ) a pair of tiny pits just inside the opening of the human nose, containing tubes lined with unique cells suspected of being pheromone detectors. Prior to 1993, it was thought humans didn't possess this "other" sense of smell and older texts will list it as found only in some reptiles and certain mammals. In snakes, this is the organ connected with the use of the tongue to taste the air; the tongue tips are brought into the mouth then inserted into the vomeronasal organ.

The author's reference to "...come up with variations..." refers back to work on the hormone testosterone, which has been shown to have the effect of lowering the threshold for aggression in some male human subjects but not others, indicating that there are individual differences in response to hormones.

over it by now.

"Anyway," Paul continued, "I've come up with a close analogue of the human pheromone that stimulates a..." he glanced at Crystal and then away, "an affectionate response."

"Do you mean sexual?" Crystal asked coolly. She could feel herself starting to blush, but not as darkly as her uncle was doing, she was sure. "I am fourteen you know."

"Not... necessarily sexual," Paul said. "We don't want to get sued for selling a product that might be accused of provoking physical assaults. We just want to create something that will make people *like* you."

"And therein lies the flaw," Dad quoted.

"Yeah. Our artificial pheromone has no scent by itself, so we'll add it to the perfumes we already manufacture. But some people like to pour on the fragrance and some only use a little dab. Getting something that will have the same effect regardless of how much you use is a tall order."

"Well, if it doesn't have a scent or anything," Crystal asked skeptically, "then how does it work?"

"There's a special organ in the tip of your nose," Uncle Paul said. He tweaked her nose and said "Honk!" Crystal just stared at him. "It's called the vomeronasal organ. It perceives the pheromone and sends a message to the brain to initiate the proper response, positive or negative."

Crystal couldn't believe that she'd once thought her uncle was cool and that his visits were both too infrequent and too short. Because tonight he was acting like a complete nerd, talking about nose organs at the dinner table for crying out loud.

"We've also got to come up with some variations. If we just tried to use one type of pheromone we might get no response at all from some people and possibly hostile reactions from others. And," Paul leaned forward, warming to his subject now, "With constant exposure even a really strong reaction can fade away to indifference or even dislike in just a few days or weeks. We've all had an experience like that. Right, Crystal?"

She gave him a weak smile in answer. "Still," Crystal said loftily, "I don't think people are that easily manipulated."

"I'll prove it to you," Paul said, rising from his chair. "Right back," he said tossing down his napkin. Then he left the room.

Mom looked at Dad, who rolled his eyes and shook his head.

Even my parents think he's a nerd, Crystal thought, wondering if she could put away enough dinner before he got back to be excused.

But when her uncle returned the whole atmosphere of the room changed. He seemed wittier and much more interesting. They lingered around the table while dishes went unwashed, TV unwatched and homework undone.

"It's ten thirty," Uncle Paul announced.

"It is?" they all said and checked their watches.

"Wow," Dad said. "Time sure flies when you're having fun."

"Well, I wish I could claim a major improvement in my social skills," Paul said. "But..." he dug a small brown bottle out of his shirt pocket and placed it on the table. "This is the real culprit. I splashed a little on before I came back." He grinned at them.

Mom and Dad looked taken aback.

But Crystal thought, *Oh, man, I've got to get some of that.*

———————

Crystal told herself when she took the little brown bottle from her uncle's shaving kit that she was field testing the stuff, even though she knew it was really just stealing. She'd been careful to pour some into an old bottle of perfume, replacing what she took out of her uncle's bottle with water. She even admitted to herself why she'd done it. Crystal wanted to see what it would be like to be really popular.

Now, two and a half weeks after her experiment began, having moved from the outermost circle looking in, to the very center of the innermost circle at school, she knew.

And she wasn't all that certain that she liked it.

The cool ones, as she and her best friend Kerri used to call them, were nice enough in their way; always on the go, ready for fun, their clothes were fantastic and they were very bright. But they were so intensely competitive that it was hard to believe that they liked each other at all. And they were always moving and changing. She was exhausted from trying to keep up with them. Not to mention broke.

Fortunately, they seemed to have suspended their rigorous judgment where she was concerned. *Due, no doubt, to the fact that they can't help but like me, she thought. But that won't last beyond the last drop of pheromone. And what, Crystal asked herself, will happen then?*

She shuddered. Their assessments were immediate and merciless. Do something uncool and you were gone.

Crystal smiled and waved to people as she moved down the corridor, walking quickly to discourage anyone from joining her. *I just want to be alone for awhile*, she thought plaintively. Popularity was a pain.

Ethical Science

The issue of ethics arises here. Ask students what they think of Paul's experimenting with his unknowing family. You can use this example from the story to move into a discussion of ethical practice in human experimentation if you wish.

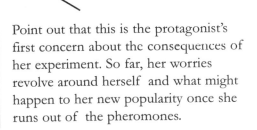

Point out that this is the protagonist's first concern about the consequences of her experiment. So far, her worries revolve around herself and what might happen to her new popularity once she runs out of the pheromones.

"Oh, hel-lo Cryssstal."

The voice was so sarcastically, syrupy sweet that Crystal didn't recognize it. She stopped and turned.

"Kerri!" she said, surprised and glad. "I've missed you." Crystal found that she meant it. She and Kerri were best friends and Kerri's dry sense of humor had always brightened her days. *What would she make of all this?* Crystal wondered, suddenly unsure if she dared confide in her friend.

"You *missed* me? Oh, ree-ly?" Kerri tipped her head in a brilliant imitation of wide-eyed brainlessness.

"Yes!" Crystal exclaimed, laughing. *I just didn't realize it until now.*

Kerri narrowed her eyes. "Well, you'd never know it," she snapped. "You've walked right by me for *two* weeks like I didn't exist. Who do you think you are anyway, Miss Stuck Up?"

Crystal blushed, but shame was quickly replaced by embarrassed irritation. "Do you have to shout?" she whispered. Joni Paine was coming towards them, walking with Paige Kipfer. "It's an experiment," she hissed at Kerri. "I can't talk here, I'll call you."

"Oh!" Kerri said her eyes widening once more. "Then I'll just run right home and sit by the phone until Miss Popularity gets around to calling me. Shall I do that? Oh, why don't I?" She glanced down the hallway and saw Joni and Paige coming towards them. Kerri turned back to glare at Crystal. "Because I've got better things to do than to wait to talk to someone I *thought* was my friend, but who is really a conceited snob." Then she spun on her heel and marched away.

"Hi, Crystal," Paige said. She glanced after Kerri, then turned and winked at Crystal. "Scraping off the losers?"

"No," Crystal said coldly. "Talking to a friend. Excuse me," she said and walked away from the two most popular girls in school.

—◆—

Crystal brooded over her conversation/spat with Kerri all afternoon. *Why was she able to be so mad at me?* Crystal wondered as she walked home. *Being close enough to be effected by the pheromone should have made her like me.* But it sure hadn't. *Oh, wait. Uncle Paul said something about getting hostile reactions.* Her lips twisted wryly. *So does this mean I'll be hated by people I like and adored by people I could care less about?* Well, that was great. She frowned. *But it's just the sort of thing Uncle Paul needs to know.*

"Hi," said a light masculine voice at her elbow.

Although Crystal had justified her theft to herself as "field testing," this is the first time in which she begins to assume the role of investigator rather than simply profiting from the result.

Crystal jumped a little in surprise. Then her jaw dropped as she looked up at the boy beside her. She didn't know who he was, but he was gorgeous; big blue eyes fringed with dark lashes, a neat, straight nose, firm jaw, full lips and jet black hair. He even had an earring.

"Sorry," he said and smiled. "I didn't mean to scare you."

Crystal could feel a sort of melting sensation as he smiled. "It's okay," she told him. "I was just... uh, thinking," she finished lamely.

"Nothing important, I hope," he said.

He had a way of looking at her that made her feel she was the most important thing in the world.

"I... No," she said, looking away from his intense gaze and blushing. "Not at all."

"I'm Brian Churchill," he said and held out his hand. "I'm new here."

"Well, I'm sure you'll fit right in," Crystal said, shaking it. *There'll be blood on the walls of the girls' locker room when they get a load of you*, she thought, reluctantly letting go of his warm palm. *Any red-blooded female would fight to get a chance at this guy.* Despite the fascinated look he was giving her, she never thought of herself as having a prayer of attracting him.

"Well, I thought I'd start on a high note by introducing myself to you," Brian told her with a smile.

Crystal was completely dazzled; she almost swallowed her tongue. He must be at least a junior, tall as he was, and she a lowly freshman. She couldn't speak for a moment, it was as though she'd forgotten what to do with the air in her lungs. "Thank you," she said, feeling like she was gushing.

"I was wondering," he said, "if you're free Friday night, if you could show me where the kids around here go to have fun."

"I'd love to," Crystal said. In the back of her mind she knew her parents wouldn't approve. Brian was a stranger and much older than she. *But like I said, any red-blooded girl would fight for this guy.*

"Great, I'll pick you up at seven."

"You have a car?" she asked.

"Sure."

My father is not going to be pleased. Her parents had never said she couldn't date. But she never had, so the subject hadn't come up. She gave him her address, telephone number, and directions.

Here the author contrasts the normal "chemistry" between two people by showing us Crystal's reaction to the attractive stranger as opposed to the stranger's response to the pheromone. This provides forewarning that the experiment is not going to produce the results Crystal wished.

Have students comment on the moment when Crystal seems to have forgotten the pheromone itself as she becomes more and more involved with its results. You can, if you wish, stop the class reading the story after Crystal says: "I'm so sorry, Kerri." and have students write their own climax. Compare results.

"See you Friday," he said. "If not before."

He looked just as good walking away, slim and graceful.

I have got to tell Kerri, she thought and practically ran home.

———————♦———————

"I don't care," Kerri said. Her voice was cold and controlled.

"But..."

"You can't just treat me like dirt for two weeks, Crystal, and then call up like nothing has happened. What sort of fool do you think I am?"

"I-I'm sorry, I never meant..."

"Then you're dumber than you're acting. And Crystal, you're acting dumb. So if you want to confide in someone, why don't you just go to your new friends? Cause I'm not interested." And she hung up.

Crystal just sat there, holding the phone to her ear as it cycled from silence, to dial tone, to the annoying squawk that warned the phone was off the hook. She felt frozen inside and very much like she wanted to cry. *Kerri is my best friend*, she protested in her mind. Tears welled in her eyes and she knew, to her shame, that sometime in the last two weeks Kerri had been crying over her.

"I'm sorry," she whispered and wiped her eyes. "I'm so sorry, Kerri."

———————♦———————

Crystal had decided the next morning that she was both too embarrassed and too upset to talk to Kerri and that she should avoid her. But now it seemed that Kerri was everywhere. In English, just one of the classes they shared, the teacher split the class into partners and she and Kerri were put together. In gym, the coach showed them stretching exercises that required two people. They were put together again.

This is ridiculous, Crystal raged inwardly as she marched down the hall to her next class. *This never happens, now, twice in one day we get teamed up.* Just two weeks ago it would have been great. *Now it's like dealing with a robot.* Or a hostile stranger. *She's really overreacting*, Crystal thought, smoldering. *It's not fair! She won't even let me explain.*

Crystal turned a corner and there was Brian. She'd spoken to him a couple of times since she'd met him on Wednesday and liked him even more now than she had at first sight. He was genuinely nice and smart too.

She lifted her head. *Well, I am not going to let Kerri spoil tonight*, she thought. With an effort of will she pushed all concerns about her runaway friend to the back of her mind.

"Hi," Brian said with a warm smile as she walked up to him. "Jeff here was telling me that Robo-Rock is the place to go on a Friday night."

Crystal nodded. "It's nice," she said.

And it was. It was an underage club, with a very good live band and excellent pizza, burgers, and fries. It served only soft drinks and was glitzy and expensive; the cover charge was fifteen bucks a head. Even so it was always crowded. The people she'd been spending time with thought nothing of going there two or three times a week.

"But it's way overpriced," she said dismissively.

"Let me worry about that," Brian said. The bell rang. "I'll see you at seven." He leaned close and said softly, "Wear a dress."

Crystal watched him walk away, exasperation marring her pleasure in the sight. *Wear a dress*, she thought. She'd been planning to, but now wasn't sure she would. *What is this? A date with a dress code? Wear a dress! Sheeesh!* She felt like yelling, "Yeah, and you wear some pants!"

Crystal was getting to the point where she didn't like taking orders from her *parents* anymore and now here was this *guy... Sheeesh!*

In the end she decided to wear a dress. *I'm not going to cut off my nose to spite my face. I want to wear a dress and I'm going to. Mature people did what they wanted*, and if that pleased the people around them, great, and it if didn't, tough.

As an afterthought she put her perfume bottle in her purse. *Just in case,* she thought. Crystal didn't pursue the idea any further. In case of what?, was something she didn't actually want to know.

Her parents told her that she looked nice, and they seemed to like Brian. But Crystal could tell that they were uneasy about letting her go. She'd known this would happen the first time she wasn't going out in a crowd.

I'm a little nervous myself, Crystal thought.

When they got out to the car, Brian said, "Thank you for wearing a dress."

"Well, I was going to anyway," she said. She almost bit her tongue off to keep from saying, "So you didn't have to order me to wear one and I'd appreciate it if you didn't do it again." *I am looking forward to tonight*, she scolded herself. *I don't think getting strident will improve the quality of the evening.*

When they got to the club she insisted on paying her own way

The social upheavals of adolescence overlap here with the interaction of the pheromones, making it increasingly difficult for the protagonist to sort out her own feelings.

cynosure - center of attraction or admiration; a guiding star

As Crystal dances, she enjoys her own natural, unaffected response to Brian. The author doesn't give her much time before starting to reveal the potential consequences of controlling the responses of others.

in.

"No," Brian said, laughing, but annoyed. "You're my date."

Crystal shifted and pursed her lips. "I'm, uh, a little uncomfortable with the idea of your paying for my company," she said quietly, so that the guy who collected the cover charge wouldn't hear. *Especially when, if you had a choice, you wouldn't accept it for free.*

Before he could say anything else, she slapped her fifteen dollars down and held out her hand to be stamped. She saw Brian's lips tighten and she smiled at him.

"C'mon," she urged after he'd been stamped too, and taking his hand dragged him into the music, the glitter, and the flashing lights.

"I love this song," he said. "Let's dance first."

She nodded eagerly and they walked onto the dance floor hand in hand. Crystal was starving, in fact, since she hadn't eaten dinner, but food could wait. She could feel the other kids looking them over as they danced. *The cynosure of all eyes*, she thought. They'd been given the word in English class this week and she'd never imagined that she'd have a use for it.

The song ended and she turned to leave. The band struck up a slow song and Brian tapped her on the shoulder. Crystal turned and he opened his arms to her. *He must have already eaten*, she thought, a bit resentfully. Her empty stomach rumbled. *I hope he doesn't notice*, Crystal thought as she stepped into his arms.

Brian pulled her close and she put her head against his chest. She was short enough that she could hear his heart beating. His hand felt as hot as a brand where it rested on her back and she felt the touch of his chin brushing her hair. Crystal inhaled deeply and felt her face curl up into a sappy smile. *Pheromones,* she thought dreamily.

"Uh, Crystal?" Brian said.

She pulled away from his chest and looked up at him inquiringly. He had the most peculiar expression on his face, like he was feeling sick and trying to hide it. *Well, no wonder he didn't want to eat*, she thought.

"Would you mind if we left?" he asked.

"Leave?" she said in disappointment. "We just got here."

He made a wry expression. "We could go somewhere quiet and... talk."

It's the pheromone, she thought desperately, *I've never been this close to anybody while I was wearing it. He doesn't like it anymore and he's embarrassed to be with me.* Brian gave her a strained smile, still holding her close as they swayed to the music. *Or maybe it's just wearing off. Who knows what its shelf life is?*

"Okay," Crystal agreed. His smile widened. "I'll just go to the ladies' room," she said and slipped out of his embrace.

———◦———

There was no one in the ladies' room when she entered. Crystal went to the little vanity shelf and dug the bottle out of her bag. She unscrewed the top and paused.

Does increasing the dose increase the effect? But if he's starting to dislike me because of it, will putting more on make him hate me? She looked up and into her eyes in the mirror. All she could think of was her uncle saying, "I've got something that will get you more love than you can handle." *Is that what's going on?* she wondered, aghast.

The door slammed open and she jumped, the pheromone leapt out of the bottle and splashed her hands and the counter. *Oh, great!* Crystal thought and reached for a tissue to wipe up the spill and her hands.

The girl who had opened the door so furiously took a deep breath. By the time she let it out she was smiling.

"Oh, I'm sorry, did I startle you?" she asked brightly.

"It's okay," Crystal said. "I was just a million miles away."

Dropping the tissue in the basket, she smiled and left, little knowing that she had just made Robo-Rock's ladies' room the place to be. No one who went in, came out, until management forced them all to leave at closing time.

Heads turned in her wake as she walked back to Brian and boys looked at him with envy and resentment. He, on the other hand, lit up as she approached and her anxieties were soothed.

———◦———

Brian drove to Lavender Lane, a dead end street with no lavender but with a great view of the city lights. It was well known at school as the local lover's lane. Crystal looked nervously out at the utter darkness around them and then back at Brian, his face eerily underlit by the dashboard lights.

This might not have been such a good idea, she thought, unsure if she meant the extra dose of pheromone or their deserted location.

Brian pulled over and turned off the engine and the lights.

"So, tell me about yourself, Brian." she asked.

He chuckled in the dark. "You sound like the guidance counselor. Only she called me young man."

Her eyes had grown accustomed to the darkness, and there was

Until this moment, Crystal has been in control of the pheromone, by applying the amount she chose. The author is now warning us that Crystal may be about to face the consequences of uncontrolled use of the substance.

Crystal's loss of control of the experiment is further emphasized by her situation with Brian, alone and in a deserted location.

frission - An emotional thrill, shiver

Recognizing Consequences

As Crystal realizes that Brian's actions are just like those of the moths, she is faced with the knowledge that she has removed Brian's free will and so his avowal of affection for her is meaningless. Not only has she failed to achieve what she wanted, she has come to recognize the power of the pheromone to "exploit" the emotional reactions of others.

enough moonlight filtering through the branches of the trees overhead to let her make out his features. His eyes sparkled as he moved towards her and Crystal's heart did a curious double leap.

Brian seized her hand and kissed it passionately, then he rubbed his cheek against it. Crystal caught her breath, a little frission of excitement tickled her skin. Then he rubbed his other cheek against her palm. Then he rubbed the first cheek over her knuckles.

She half frowned.

Brian took her by the wrist and stroked her hand over his face. His eyes were closed and there was this weird little smile on his face. Then he began to make little grunting sounds of contentment.

Ee-yuk! Crystal thought and gave her hand a tug. Brian opened his eyes and looked at her with happy bemusement. Then with a little sigh he laid his cheek against her hand again, looking like he intended to stay that way all night.

Boy, Crystal thought, horror-struck, *too much of that stuff is... too much.* She had a sudden vision of her classmates and even herself wandering the halls of the high school blissed out and foolish, drawn after this one and that, helpless to resist the chemical overtures surrounding them.

Brian kissed her knuckles and sniffed them, reminding her of that gypsy moth trap her father had bought and the moths that had fluttered around his fingers where he'd touched the bait. *This is just as bad.* Crystal bit her lip. *No, it's worse. I feel like the wicked witch who's put a spell on the prince.* Well, maybe not. The wicked witch probably wouldn't feel as guilty as she did. Tears of shame rose in her eyes.

"Take me home," she said.

Brian looked up at her. "Already?" he asked. "We just got here."

"Please," Crystal said, squeezing her words past the lump in her throat. "I want to go home." She snatched her hand away. "I don't want to exploit you, Brian."

He grinned. "You can exploit me if you want to. I don't mind."

Crystal shook her head violently. "You wouldn't if you kn-knew," she managed to say. "Y-you'd ha-ha-hate me."

He leaned closer and put his hand on her shoulder. "No, I wouldn't. I like you, Crystal."

That did it. She burst into floods of tears. Crystal could barely get her breath and cried, most unattractively, with her mouth wide open. Through her tears she caught sight of Brian's face and his expression made her laugh. Then she couldn't stop, either laughing or crying, and she began to get frightened.

"I-I can't s-stop," she choked out. She shook her head helplessly and laughed and cried and shrugged.

Brian started the car and took her home, silently giving her nervous little glances as he drove. He let her out at the curb and then took off without waiting to see if she got in all right.

Crystal ran up the stairs, knowing that her parents would be alarmed, but not wanting to expose them to the massive overdose of pheromone she was wearing. She slipped out of her shoes and jumped into the shower fully dressed.

"Crystal?" her mother said, knocking on the door. "Honey? Is everything all right."

Sure, Mom," Crystal said. "You can come in."

When her mother stepped inside the bathroom, Crystal pulled the shower curtain aside partway.

"What a mess," she said, managing to grin. "We just sat down at our table when someone bumped into a waiter and he dropped a whole pitcher of coke on us. Poor Brian got the worst of it." She looked out at her mother. "Sorry to run by you like that, but I couldn't wait to get the gunk off."

"I can see that," her mother said, gazing in wonder at her fully clad, soaking wet daughter. She smiled weakly. "What a shame about your...date."

Crystal shook her head and wrung out her skirt. "Nah. It wasn't really a date, Mom." She smiled. "Any supper left? I'm starving."

"I'll see what I can find." Her mother sounded puzzled.

"Thanks, Mom."

Crystal sat at her desk in her bathrobe and wrote:

Dear Uncle Paul,
I took some of the pheromone from the bottle in your shaving kit and replaced it with water. I must admit that I used it. And it worked. But I'm ashamed of myself for using it at all. It's not right to force people to like you. The very least a person should be allowed is the right to choose their friends. Think of how you'd feel if someone was using this stuff on you. And if it goes on the market, they will. Personally, I'd rather be disliked than turn someone I liked into a zombie. So I hope you will stop making this stuff.

I'm really sorry,
Crystal

The End

The day after?
Suggest this as a starting point for a story by students. Some may choose to have sinister forces discover Crystal's experiment etc. Others may produce more personal pieces about how Crystal does (or does not) succeed in repairing her own place with the school's social structure without the pheromone. If you wish, use students' stories as a framework when discussing the themes of ethics and human experimentation further.

After reading and summarizing *Love is Chemistry*, you may wish to hold a class debate on the pros and cons of this statement: "Research into substances with the potential to modify human behavior must be stopped."

Stirling, Jan

Jan's short fiction can be found in science fiction and fantasy anthologies and magazines, including: "Werewench" in *Chicks in Chainmail*, ed. Esther Friesner, Baen Books (1996).

Jan's Top Three

"Let's see. I'd recommend anything by Andre Norton. *Warrior's Apprentice* by Lois McMaster Bujold. And I'm especially fond of Poul Anderson's *Brain Wave*."

Meet Jan Stirling

❝Why did I become a writer?" Jan Stirling smiles. "When you're around writers all the time, you can't help yourself. You want to tell stories too." Jan credits her blossoming career as a writer to the influence of her husband Steve, author of several SF and Fantasy books under the name S.M. Stirling. "Steve reads my work and I read his. We encourage each other, but what's even more important, we recognize each other's writing strengths and weaknesses. It's an ongoing give and take that improves both our work. And I'm learning all the time."

"...to me the greatest pleasure is in challenging myself..."

Jan's desire to learn is part of her nature. "I've always been a craftsperson," she notes. "For example, I like sewing. But to me the greatest pleasure is in challenging myself to do more. So I enjoy making costumes that are accurate as well as beautiful."

"The more I write, the more I enjoy it."

As her interest in writing grew, Jan became involved in writers' groups. "Steve was always a great help, but I wanted as much criticism as possible." The writers' groups tutored her in the basics and she set herself strict goals to follow their suggestions. "At the time, it wasn't easy to show others my work," Jan confesses. "And I find my earliest efforts actually painful to read now. But I'm glad I had the courage to get started. The more I write, the more I enjoy it."

"...A bestseller!"

What's ahead? "More writing! A bestseller!" grins Jan. "And I'm learning how to renovate. We've bought a house, our first, and I'm determined to make it just right." Based on Jan's approach to everything she does, it seems very likely to happen.

What if...

Lesson Suggestions

The author, Jan Stirling, was born and raised in New England, but has travelled extensively across North America. She lived for several years in Toronto, Canada, before settling in New Mexico. A mentor and friend to many writers, Jan and her husband Steve attend several science fiction and fantasy conventions each year in order to renew acquaintances and share ideas.

Lesson: Encouraging Creativity

Have students read this story, then use the worksheet *A Letter of Concern* (pg 58) as a guide to writing their own letter regarding an issue of interest. You can elicit ideas on issues from the class, then choose one issue for all. This is a good approach if the issue is one that affects your community and/or students directly. Alternatively, have students come up with their own issue and do the assignment as homework.

Warm-up

Homework

Lesson: Critical Reading Skills

Divide students into small groups. Have each group come to a decision as to the author's attitude towards one of the following issues or topics presented in this story. Their decision must be supported by one or more examples drawn from the story. Once they have done so, lead a class discussion on what the author is like and how her views affect the science as shown here.

Group

- Human experimentation (without consent)
- Human experimentation (with consent)
- Popularity
- Free will
- Teen sexuality
- Self-esteem
- Cosmetic industry

Lesson: Popular Views of Science and Scientists

Have students read this story, then discuss the role of peer pressure in shaping someone's opinion of themselves and others. Follow by having students use the worksheet, *I Want to Believe! Survey* (pg 59) to collect information on sources of information considered credible. Discuss the results. Do not permit students to express scorn or disbelief at the choices made by others.

Recommended Materials:
- a copy of the companion anthology, *Packing Fraction and Other Tales of Science & Imagination* per student.
- information on issues, including addresses if you wish students to send their letters.
- other materials will vary depending on the chosen activity.

Where to find It:
If you do not have copies of the student anthology, several of the activities here can be used with other science fiction stories or on their own. Consult the list of recommended works starting on page 120.

Survey Activity
See page 59 for a suggestion to have students conduct a survey concerning the relative weights given to the opinions of scientists, non-scientist professionals, and non-professionals when considering a science-based issue.

If possible, show and contrast exposé-style documentaries and articles (such as alien autopsies) with more credible examples.

There are additional lesson ideas on page 60.

ships were deemed hazardous to the oceans and banned?

A Letter of Concern

(Your name and address.)

(The name and address of the person who will read your letter.)

(The Date)

Re: _____
(The subject of your letter goes here.)

Dear *(The person's name if possible)*

Your first paragraph should contain a sentence to identify *who* you are, a sentence to identify *what* is of concern to you, and a sentence to explain *why* you chose to send this letter. (Hint: This is good place to mention how or where you found this person's name.)

If your letter is a request for action on an issue:
Your second and possibly third paragraphs should state your position calmly and clearly. For example, if you are writing to alert a government agency about toxic waste near your school, you would use these paragraphs to say how you found out about the waste, why you believe it poses a threat, and any suggestions you have on how to deal with this problem. (Hint: Do not be abusive, sarcastic, or threatening. You want to enlist this person or agency's assistance. You also want to be seen as honestly looking for solutions, not hunting a target for blame.)

If your letter is a request for information on an issue:
Use these paragraphs to describe the information you seek. Try to be as precise as possible and ask no more than three questions in one letter. Be sure to mention if you are supplying an SASE (self-addressed stamped envelope) for the person's response to you. (Hint: Providing an SASE increases your chances of a quick response dramatically.)

Your final paragraph should thank the person for his or her attention. You may also emphasize how important this issue is to you.

Yours truly,
(your signature)

• ALIEN AUTOPSIES • COLD FUSION •
• HUMAN CLONES • CHEMICAL WARFARE •
• LONGEVITY DRUG AT LAST •

What to believe? Every day you face a flood of information about science-based issues. Some ideas appear more science fiction than fact, but the truth is often stranger than we can imagine. The only sure way is to gather as much information as you can, from a variety of sources you feel are reliable, then make your own informed decisions. It's a time-consuming process, and many people prefer to trust one or more sources to do that checking for them, such as the nightly news broadcast or national newspaper.

But what happens when the sources we trust are copied by those we otherwise wouldn't trust? Some television documentaries and shows collect viewers (and advertising revenue) by playing on our worst fears, with reports that appear perfectly authentic until you read the credits or disclaimers at the end. There have been shows, meant purely for entertainment, so believable that the filmmakers themselves can't convince some viewers that they were fooled.

Conduct this survey in your school or community. Be sure to check with your teacher before you proceed.

"Hello. I'm conducting a survey on sources of information. When I read you the names of the following issues, please tell me which source you would trust most to give you the correct information."

◉ **Cancer cures**
television, national newspaper, government bulletin, other (please specify) _____

◉ **UFO sightings**
television, national newspaper, government bulletin, other (please specify) _____

◉ **Global warming**
television, national newspaper, government bulletin, other (please specify) _____

◉ **Flu epidemic**
television, national newspaper, government bulletin, other (please specify) _____

survey: def'n. take or present a general view; the general view or consideration of something.

I Want to Believe! Survey

Additional Lesson Ideas - *Love is Chemistry*

Lesson: Diffusion of Substances

Have students read this story as a followup to your activities concerning the diffusion of substances, particularly through the air. If you wish, use perfumes to demonstrate diffusion. Students could then extend this investigation into an examination of the the relative rates of diffusion of various fragrances. (Another interesting option for students is the fragrance associated with breath mints or chewing gums.)

Lesson: Ethical Standards in Science

After reading and discussing this story, have students draw up a suggested list of ethical standards for scientific experimentation. (Decide beforehand if you wish this list to be all-inclusive or to focus on human experimentation.) You can also combine this activity with preparations for a school science fair, using the resulting list of standards as part of the requirements for entry. See marginal note.

Lesson: The Science of Persuasion

Use this story as a starting point for individual or group projects on consumer information regarding personal care products. Whether students perform experiments to compare products and assess the validity of claims made on their behalf or not, they should be able to compare the information supplied in the following terms:

- Presentation: Is the information clearly written and easily understood?
- Verification of Claims: Is it possible to verify any claims regarding scientific testing or results? (For example, is there a mailing address and/or name of a reputable scientific organization supplied with the information?)
- Lack of Verification: Are there any claims about the product which are impossible to verify? How important are these claims to the purchaser of the product?
- Product History: Has this product appeared in any other form or under another label? Were the same claims made? (This information can sometimes be obtained by asking older relatives or a pharmacist.)

Ethical Standards

While you want students to produce their own list for the class, it can be useful to have a copy of a list such as the one used by your own science department, National Academy of Sciences (US), National Research Council (Can.), or other organizations available to demonstrate to students the widespread and important nature of such guidelines in science.

What if...

Speculative Verse, Art, and Other Media

"...I am Newtonian..."

from *Much Slower than Light*
by Carolyn Clink

Time Travel

This is one of the most familiar — and popular — "what if's" in science fiction. Here, Carolyn is playing with various views of time itself by stating a preference for the Newtonian approach in which time is linear. The terms "much slower than light," "frame of reference," "twin paradox," "atomic clocks," all refer to Einstein's special relativity and its more complex and encompassing view of time. Since a person lives much slower than light, it might be assumed relativity is of concern to only a very few. The phrase "steady state" is a reference to the Steady State Theory, in which the universe is neither expanding nor contracting. In Carolyn's own words: "As outdated as Newton, but just as comforting!"

Website

See page 118 for a site about Sir Isaac Newton.

Where to find it:
A superb resource on relativity for students is Ernie McFarland's *Einstein's Special Relativity: Discover it for yourself*, 1998 Trifolium Books Inc.

Much Slower than Light

I am Newtonian.
My frame of reference
is my frame of preference.

A pox on your twin paradox
and your atomic clocks.

It's too much of a bother
being my own grandfather.
I'll just stay home and wait
in my own steady state.

by Carolyn Clink

Changing Sex in Mid Ocean

In mid life, mid ocean,
out for a refreshing swim,
suddenly I'm a colorful
he-fish, wet oxygen
squeezing through my blue
gills.

Proud resident of a mini
coral Balmoral — I'm mating,
not dating, no flowers
no long-term commitments.
Just me and the water.
I don't like this page
out of Darwin,
there's no romance here.

by Carolyn Clink

Personal Responses
The ability of some fish species to change sex took considerable time to be accepted as a possibility but was ultimately confirmed by observation. In this piece, Carolyn is doing more than revealing this new bit of knowledge — she is giving her response to what it would be like to have the same biological switch happen to her as a human being. This is an excellent "what if..." for students to use as story premise. James A. Gardner's novel, *Commitment Hour*, explores this premise in a society where humans choose their permanent sex after experiencing alternating periods as male or female from birth through adolescence.

Myth and Lore
Encourage students to learn the meanings of the terms used in this poem in order to appreciate how Carolyn is applauding the work of molecular chemists in creating these new, large forms of carbon by comparing their achievements to magic.

Buckyball: refers to the geodesic dome invented by architect R. Buckminster Fuller. The name buckminster-fullerene (and nickname "buckyball") was adopted for the recently discovered third form of carbon molecule, a round, hollow, cagelike structure with extraordinary stability. This class of carbon molecules, including C_{60}, are called **fullerenes** and have characteristics which suit them for many purposes, ranging from lubricants to superconductors.

Alchemy: the earliest form of chemistry, connected with the intent of transmuting one substance, such as lead, into something of more value, such as gold.

Superconducting: able to conduct electricity with almost perfect efficiency, i.e. no resistance.

Hex: a spell or magical curse

Waxing, waning: refer to the cycles of the moon.

Nobel: the Nobel prize for science as well as play on the word "noble."

New Moon

The moon is a Buckyball
filled with myth and lore,
The alchemy of pentagons
opens a superconducting door,
A transmutation hex
on carbon-60, -70, or more,
Waxing, waning, or fullerene
it's Nobel to the core.

by Carolyn Clink

Meet Carolyn Clink

Astronomy and poetry. Carolyn Clink's interests suit her perfectly to writing science fiction verse. "I look up at the sky as often as I can," she says. "It's not a cold remote place to me."

Carolyn studied astrophysics after high school. "But I preferred being outside to see the stars. And I wasn't strong in physics."

Carolyn focused on her other interest, language, and now works for a printing company. "We do many of the advertising flyers you'll find in your newspaper." It's demanding. "We must meet the advertisers' schedule as well as the newspapers'."

Her poetry is an essential part of her life outside work. "I don't write it all the time," she laughs. "But when I'm inspired, off I'll go."

"...there's a lot going on in those few words."

"I like to keep it simple and short," says Carolyn. "But there's a lot going on in those few words. I prefer to not take things very seriously. At the same time, I want to place elements together in a new way. I need words capable of expressing what I feel."

"Blank paper can really scare me."

Carolyn is not always confident. "Blank paper can really scare me," she agrees. "I want to write something fresh and new. I worry that I'll repeat myself or do something similar to what's been done, so I try to read as many poems by others as I can."

Carolyn sells her poetry in several markets. "There's a lot of interest in science fiction poetry, but I sell mainstream and even horror, too." Carolyn also edits science fiction short stories with her husband, author Robert J. Sawyer. "And we are both amateur astronomers," she smiles. "So I guess I'm still following my interests after all."

Carolyn's Top Three

"I recommend *Where Late The Sweet Birds Sang* by Kate Wilhelm, *Falling Free* by Lois McMaster Bujold, and *Inherit the Stars* by James P. Hogan."

Clink, Carolyn

Tesseracts6, ed. with Robert J. Sawyer, Tesseract Books (1997) (an anthology of Canadian science fiction and fantasy)

Carolyn Clink's speculative poetry has appeared in *Analog*, *Northern Frights*, *On Spec*, and *TransVersions*.

Since this biography was prepared, Carolyn has left the advertising business to act as publicist and assistant for her husband, science fiction author Robert J. Sawyer. Their first joint project, editing *Tesseracts6*, was proof this was a decision sure to please Carolyn's readers as well.

Larry's Top Three

"My number one is Jules Verne's *20,000 Leagues Under the Sea*, but if you want to read an English version true to Verne's original ask for the one by Miller and Walter in 1993 (US Naval Institute Press ISBN 1-55750-877-1). It's worth it!

"I need three more? *War of the Worlds*, H.G. Wells, Arthur C. Clarke's *Childhood's End* and *The Chrysalids* by John Wyndham." And, since starting this project I've read Rob Sawyer's *Starplex*. Definitely add it to my list!"

A Challenge from Larry

"I'm fond of putting a little something extra into each of my illustrations. I take an element of the story and hide it in the body of the picture for the reader to find. It may represent an idea, an emotion, or an artifact — something tangible. Unfortunately, I can't reveal what these are in the context of the illustrations for the five stories [in Packing Fraction*]; that would ruin all my fun, and yours. I have found that discovering these hidden elements really increases the reader's enjoyment of the whole process. So, good luck finding my "secret toy-surprises" as I like to call them."*

Meet Larry Stewart

Larry carries with him a small, leather-bound notebook. If you are lucky, he'll show you what's inside. "I keep track of ideas, events, and images here," he says, flipping the pages. Intricate drawings wind their way up each one. But the beautiful script seems in another language, until you hold it up to a mirror. Larry grins. "I actually write faster and neater using mirror-writing. Being left-handed it has always seemed a more natural way to move my hand." He pauses. "And I like to keep my notes and thoughts private."

"I work in whatever media best suits the piece, and the needs of my clients...."

Larry's approach to his art is just as thoughtful. "Each piece deserves my best," he says seriously. He takes his time, thinking about the right image and the right approach. "I work in whatever media best suits the piece, and the needs of my clients. For this book, I used pen and ink." Although Larry decided on the image he wanted to use to illustrate each story, he faxed his preliminary drawings to the editor and authors. "My long-time mentor and friend, artist Frank Kelly Freas, said something to me I've never forgotten," Larry explains. "'Illustration is art in service to the story.' I want my illustrations to do just that."

...the passion to create.

Since he was young, Larry has drawn what he sees — and doesn't confine himself to just using his eyes. "I love telescopes and microscopes." He feels the prime characteristic of an illustrator is the passion to create. "This is work you have to do. There's no choice for an artist." He smiles. "And no greater pleasure."

Let Me Draw You a Picture

Advice to Aspiring Illustrators from Larry Stewart
❝When an author writes a story, he or she weaves a world in words. As an illustrator, it is my great pleasure to take those words and create a visual image of a moment in space and time. I thought it might be helpful for any aspiring illustrators if I described the process I follow.

What if...

"A successful illustration takes a scene or a moment of drama and shows it in such a way as to catch the attention and curiosity of a potential reader. The art on a book cover is trying to make you notice that book among other contenders.

"Interior illustrations have a different role. These images give a visual reality to the story, comprised of: mood, identity, and form. Mood sets the emotional tone for the story's action, while identity gives a face or shape to the character(s). Form gives shape to the scenery in which the story is taking place. What does the ship look like? How does the planet appear at sunset? All these things and many more come into play when rendering visually the author's world.

"The first step is to read the story. Certain scenes will stick in your mind and form an image. It's vital, however, to never give away the ending. The mood will present itself and you will know whether it is a dark grim realm or a happy one, or something in-between. Once I have these criteria, I do a sketch. I study this and think of the story. I ask myself: Does it set the mood? Is this the right pose for the character in the scene? I re-read the story for any new ideas or insights to add to the sketch, removing any images that do not work.

"Be sure to do your research. Ignorance of the facts has killed many an otherwise good illustration. For example, if the story takes place in Medieval times, don't use armor from the Renaissance. A good illustrator also learns the forms of everyday objects. Who knows when a humble glass bottle will be the focus of an entire picture? (See "Love is Chemistry.") You are trying to give the universe visual form and identity. You have to know the forms before giving the essence.

"I follow what I call Stewart's Rule: "The illustrator draws what the author would if he or she could draw." When I accept any illustrating job, I consider it my responsibility to give the client what they want, not what I think they should have. If they impose restrictions, that just gives me the chance to be even more creative. It hones my skills and makes me a better, more creative illustrator!

"I wish everyone out there the best of luck. Illustrating is one of the most exciting fields there is and it requires the very best you can deliver, so never give anything but your best ideas and creative spark. I've drawn you a picture of what's involved, now you draw one of your own as you see it.

"Cheers!"

"Illustration is one of the most fascinating forms of the visual arts. To draw a picture that captures your own vision is one thing, but to capture in lines and shade the vision of someone else from their written description is quite another."

"My main aim in each illustration is to tease the reader with an image that fits the story, but one that will only become clear after the reader finishes the story. This makes the illustration pleasing to the reader and increases their enjoyment of the story and the reading experience."

"Even after assembling all the elements for the illustration and finishing the preliminary work, problems can occur. While doing the illustration for "Ancient Dreams," I had represented the Matriarch Acara as a young woman with strong, noble features. As I re-read the story, I realized that Acara was old and changed the illustration accordingly."

a drug let people breathe underwater?

Where to find it:
Speculative verse can be found in many science fiction magazines. See the list of recommended titles starting on page 120.

Warm-up

Website

See page 119 for sites of interest to poets.

While mainstream poets often struggle to find an audience, those writing speculative verse, whether science fiction, fantasy, or horror, have had reasonably accessible markets particularly within magazines and anthologies.

Speculative Verse

One of the things I most enjoy about speculative verse is the level of understanding needed to use scientific ideas and terms in a deceptively short and simple-looking piece of writing. However, asking students to produce poetry based on science fiction can be an interesting exercise. I've found it very successful and motivating as an option for individual students, especially those students adamantly not interested in science. Whether it works as effectively for an entire class appears to depend largely on the particular class. You will be the best judge.

I've found the following activities work well for grade 9 (or younger) students and for students in their final year, leading me to wonder if this is a reflection of the concurrent program in language arts at those levels and/or the willingness of these students to take a few risks in front of their peers.

Activity: What if _____ hadn't been invented?
- Have students think of a scientific discovery that affects them personally. (Alternatively, an item of technology.)
- Ask them to imagine "what if this discovery hadn't occurred?"
- Have them write a short poem to describe how their lives — or society as a whole — might change based on this premise.

Activity: Hypothetical Verse
As an exercise in creativity, have students propose an hypothesis for an experiment in verse rather than prose. They can use a limerick, simple free verse, or even haiku structure.

Activity: Valid Vocabulary
- Using Carolyn Clink's verse as an example, have students create their own verse which must include as many related scientific terms as possible.
- To promote a wider range of terms, have students consult text glossaries or pull unfamiliar terms from a popular science article and define them within the body of verse.

Extension Opportunities
- Link vocabulary development with writing skills by having students prepare verses to use as signs for the different scientific disciplines at a science fair or parent/teacher night.
- Publish student poetry on the school or class website (or as part of a science newsletter).
- Make students aware of upcoming poetry contests and/or host one in the science/language arts departments of your school.
- Invite a published poet from your community to conduct a writing workshop as part of science class.

What if...

Speculative Illustration

With the exception of children's literature, few other genres approach science fiction for the wealth of illustration involved at every level. From book covers to computer game graphics, from magazine and comic illustration to images on screen, the work of science fiction (and fantasy) illustrators remains in steady demand.

Many science fiction illustrators work as science illustrators and vice versa. For example, several members on the design team at NASA worked on 3-dimensional renderings of Star Trek's *Enterprise* (Paramount) for posters and books. Babylon 5 and other shows have featured Hubble telescope images.

Regardless of where or why, the art of illustrating science concepts requires attention to detail as well as imagination and craftmanship. Here are just a few opportunities to blend illustrating with science in meaningful ways in class.

Activity: Build an Alien

Conduct a technology/design exercise in which students are supplied with (or choose) a particular environment then within those constraints produce a model of a biologically-feasible alien lifeform. If you wish, have students work in groups to design several components of an alien food web. (The worksheet, *Alien Construction* (pg 86) may be helpful.)

Activity: Accuracy Counts

Have students draw, by hand or computer, the laboratory setup for an experiment. Stipulate the following:
- The drawing must show all components to scale.
- There should be clear labels so that another person can correctly assemble the apparatus using only the drawing. For example, every piece of equipment should be named and any methods of joining or clamping clearly indicated.

Activity: Illustrating a Story

Have students illustrate a science fiction story or popular science article. They must be able to cite the source of their illustration, including the passage they have chosen.

Extension Opportunities

- Use student illustrations to mark the contents of supply cupboards in the classroom or as signs during fairs etc.
- Have students illustrate a quote from a science fiction source as a notebook title page.
- Encourage students to design a computer game or game scenario based on a scientific "what if.." premise.

Recommended Materials:
- Sample book covers and illustrations - as broad a variety as possible.
- Access to art supplies (option: access to a computer with drawing software)

Recommended Student Product:
Note: students should be able to provide the source, print or otherwise, of the material they are illustrating.
- book cover for a novel (possibly presented as a wrap around an existing book)
- magazine cover
- advertisement for a book or movie
- illustration for a scene
- background for a computer game scenario
- t-shirt or other wearable art
- illustration of a starship or other technology from a story

---

How times have changed...
A fun exercise is to have students compare the cover art used for the same book at different times and to draw conclusions about society, publishing, and the level of science expected of the readership. Several publishers are now reprinting classic science fiction authors with modern covers, providing an ideal opportunity for this type of analysis.

Turnabout Challenge
Once students produce an illustration, have other students who are unfamiliar with the source material create their own science fiction story based on the artwork..

---

you woke up to find yourself the only person on Earth?

Indiana Jones

It was Harrison Ford playing the daredevil archeologist Indiana Jones in "Raiders of the Lost Ark" (1981) who first smashed Hollywood stereotypes of scientists as deranged or nerds.

Anime

Anime, or Japanese animation, consists of films and series dealing with almost any imaginable topic, including science fiction and/or fantasy. If you are unfamiliar with anime, but wish to use it with your class, be aware that much of the science fiction in particular is aimed at adult viewers and preview the film.

> **Where to find it:**
> * There are non-fiction titles about Star Trek on pg 117.
> * Recommended film list on pg 120.

The Source

The recent anthology *Reel Stuff*, ed. Martin H. Greenberg, DAW Books, contains short stories that were made into famous science fiction films. It can be the basis of a valuable class activity to compare movie and literary versions.

Gaming

If you are fortunate enough to have computer gamers in your classroom, you can enlist them as a resource to do the following investigations:

* Rank five popular science fiction-based games by the credibility of the science used.
* Decide which of the current games portray alien races or worlds as truly different from humans and Earth. How did you decide?
* Many on-line games allow participants to develop their own scenario for an existing game and submit it to become part of the game itself. Have the class work on a science-based scenario to add to such a game.

Other Media

Many of your students will be more familiar with other media representations of science fiction than literature. These include:
* comics and graphic novels
* television series (animated, or live action)
* feature films (animated or live action)
* gaming (computer-based, videogames, live action roleplay)

Activity: Comics or Graphic Novel Study

Have students choose a science fiction-based comic or graphic novel character, for example: Spiderman or Wolverine, and use examples to show how science is a key element in stories with this character. Would the story would work as well without that science? How much science background do the writers assume in their audience?

Activity: The Science of Star Trek

Of all the science fiction on television, none have the wealth of resource material available on their background "science" as Star Trek. Interested students can explore how the writers extrapolate their what ifs? in a plot, or examine one aspect of future technology as presented by the shows and films.

Activity: Movies - Reviewing the Science

* Have students write a movie review of a film with a science-related plot. They should critique the portrayal of any scientists as well as the credibility of the science presented.
* If you wish, have students compare an older film with a newer one and answer: "Has there been a change in the film stereotype of a scientist? Are scientists now "cool, sexy, and intriguing?"

Activity: Movies - Changing Demons

Have students visit a video rental store (with permission) and survey the films available. Generate a list, by date, to see how every few years, new scientific "demons" came from the film industry, from environmental disasters to cosmic collisions, in part as reflections of current concerns. (Do not assume your students are aware of Cold War paranoia and its results. In my experience, most students are not.)

Activity: Movies - Same Science; Different Story

Have students compare films dealing with a similar science-related issue, such as *Dante's Peak* and *Volcano*. Rate these movies based on their use of the science in the story. (Another interesting choice is the various versions of *King Kong*.)

What if...

Speculating about Issues in Biology

"...We've found it...And it's no meteorite..."

from *Stream of Consciousness*
by Robert J. Sawyer

Larry Stewart encountered two challenges in illustrating this story. First, the alien's physical description required the illustrator not only to think through the anatomy of an six-limbed figure but to place that figure sitting in a particular style of chair. Secondly, Larry had decided to include one of the key story elements, the depiction of the Pythagorean Theorem.

The shape and posture of the alien took some experimentation, but Larry and the author were soon satisfied. The geometry of the theorem, however, took an additional period of careful refinement to produce this final version.

Stream of Consciousness

by Robert J. Sawyer

The roar of the helicopter blades pounded in Raji's ears — he wished the university could afford a hoverjet. The land below was rugged Canadian Shield. Pine trees grew where there was soil; lichen and moss covered the Precambrian rocks elsewhere. Raji wore a green parka, its hood down. He continued to scan the ground, and —

There! A path through the wilderness, six metres wide and perhaps half a kilometre long: trees knocked over, shield rocks scraped clean, and, at the end of it —

Incredible. Absolutely incredible.

A large dark-blue object, shaped like an arrowhead.

Raji pointed, and the pilot, Tina Chang, banked the copter to take it in the direction he was indicating. Raji thumbed the control for his microphone. "We've found it," he said, shouting to be heard above the noise of the rotor. "And it's no meteorite." As the copter got closer, Raji could see that the front of the arrowhead was smashed in. He paused, unsure what to say next. Then: "I think we're going to need the air ambulance from Sudbury."

•◆•

Raji Sahir was an astronomer with Laurentian University. He hadn't personally seen the fireball that streaked across the Ontario sky last night, flanked by northern lights, but calls about it had flooded the university. He'd hoped to recover a meteorite intact; meteors were a particular interest of his, which is why he'd come to Sudbury from Vancouver twenty years ago, in 1969. Sudbury was situated on top of an ancient iron-nickel meteorite; the city's economy had traditionally been based on mining this extraterrestrial metal.

The helicopter set down next to the dark-blue arrowhead. There could be no doubt: it was a spaceship, with its hull streamlined for reentry. On its port side were white markings that must have been lettering, but they were rendered in an alphabet of triangular characters unlike anything Raji had ever seen before.

Raji was cross-appointed to the biology department; he taught a class called "Life on Other Worlds," which until this

Reading Level

Accessible to most high school students. The presentation of the science is targeted at students in their 1st or 2nd year of science rather than more experienced students, however, to fully appreciate the story, students need a rudimentary understanding of the respiratory and circulatory systems.

What if...

For this story, the author was asked to speculate on some area of biology, particularly human biology. The author decided to speculate on how a knowledge of human physiology might be useful in interpreting the physiology of a non-human entity.

If you wish, use this story to consolidate a unit on human physiology or as a bridge between considering different body systems, such as circulation and respiration.

The idea of being "cross-appointed" may be new to students, who often view scientists as compartmentalized by field. You may wish to point out how having a broad range of knowledge, such as a dual specialty, can be immensely helpful in any area. For example, an electrical engineer I know switched into medicine and is using the training from both fields to make important advances treating mental illness with devices he was able to design and test himself.

Stream of Consciousness by Robert J. Sawyer

Taking Precautions

The author is careful to show that the protagonist, Raji, is taking what safety precautions are available as he approaches the alien craft. You may wish to have students consider what further precautions they might have taken. In the end, the potential risks have to be balanced against the unlikelihood of being completely prepared in an emergency situation. Ask students what the decision of Raji to proceed tells us about his character.

NASA has always taken the threat of carrying microorganisms to other worlds seriously. Have students investigate the precautions taken to ensure that no Earth-based organisms travelled to Mars on the Pathfinder Mission. They might also be interested in reading some of the newspaper articles that came out when the first astronauts orbited the Earth and when the first lunar landing took place. Many of these cited serious concerns about the risk of bringing non-terrestrial germs back to Earth.

moment had been completely theoretical. He and Tina clambered out of the copter, and they moved over to the landing craft. Raji had a Geiger counter with him; he'd expected to use it on a meteorite, but he waved it over the ship's hull as he walked around it. The clicks were infrequent; nothing more than normal background radiation.

When he got to the pointed bow of the lander, Raji gasped. The damage was even more severe than it looked from above. The ship's nose was caved in and crumpled, and a large, jagged fissure was cut deep into the hull. If whatever lifeforms were inside didn't already breathe Earth-like air, they were doubtless dead. And, of course, if the ship carried germs dangerous to life on Earth, well, they were already free and in the air, too. Raji found himself holding his breath, and —

"Professor!"

It was Tina's voice. Raji hurried over to her. She was pointing at a rectangular indentation in the hull, set back about two centimetres. In its centre was a circular handle.

A door.

"Should we go inside?" asked Tina.

Raji looked up at the sky. Still no sign of the air ambulance. He thought for a moment, then nodded: "First, though, please get the camcorder from the helicopter."

The woman nodded, hustled off to the chopper, and returned a moment later. She turned on the camera, and Raji leaned in to examine the door's handle. It was round, about twenty centimetres across. A raised bar with fluted edges crossed its equator. Raji thought perhaps the fluting was designed to allow fingers to grip it — but, if so, it had been built for a six-fingered hand.

He grasped the bar, and began to rotate it. After he'd turned it through 180 degrees, there was a sound like four gunshots. Raji's heart jumped in his chest, but it must have been restraining bolts popping aside; the door panel — shorter and wider than a human door — was suddenly free, and falling forward toward Raji. Tina surged in to help Raji lift it aside and set it on the ground. The circular handle was likely an emergency way of opening the panel. Normally, it likely slid aside into the ship's hull; Raji could see a gap on the right side of the opening that looked like it would have accommodated the door.

Raji and Tina stepped inside. Although the outer hull was opaque, the inner hull seemed transparent — Raji could see the gray-blue sky vaulting overhead. Doubtless there were all kinds of equipment in between the outer and inner hulls, so the image was perhaps conveyed inside via bundles of fibre optics, mapping points on the exterior to points on the interior. There was plenty of light; Raji and Tina followed the short corridor from the door into the ship's main habitat, where —

Tina gasped.

Raji felt his eyes go wide.

There was an alien being, dead or unconscious, slumped over in a bowl-shaped chair in the bow of the ship. The fissure Raji had seen outside came right through here as a wide gap in the hull; a cool breeze was blowing in from outside.

Raji rushed over to the strange creature. There was, at once, no doubt in his mind that this creature had come from another world. It was clearly a vertebrate — it had rigid limbs, covered over with a flexible greenish-gray hide. But every vertebrate on Earth had evolved from the same basic body plan, an ancestral creature with sensory organs clustered around the head, and four limbs. Oh, there were creatures that had subsequently dispensed with some or all of the limbs, but there were no terrestrial vertebrates with more than four.

But this creature had *six* limbs, in three pairs. Raji immediately thought of the ones at the top of the tubular torso as arms, and the much thicker ones at the bottom as legs. But he wasn't sure what the ones in the middle, protruding halfway between hips and shoulders, should be called. They were long enough that if the creature bent over, they could serve as additional legs, but they ended in digits complex and supple enough that it seemed they could also be used as hands.

Raji counted the digits — there were indeed six at the end of each limb. Earth's ancestral vertebrate had five digits, not six, and no Earthly animal had ever evolved with more than five. The alien's digits were arranged as four fingers flanked on either side by an opposable thumb.

The alien also had a head protruding above the shoulders — at least that much anatomy it shared with terrestrial forms. Overall, the alien had about the same bulk as Raji himself did, but its head was only the size of a grapefruit, ridiculously small for an intelligent creature. There were two things that might have been eyes covered over by lids that closed vertically; there were two ears, as well, but they were located on top of the head, and were triangular in shape, like the ears of a fox.

Although the alien was strapped into its seat, a large hunk of hull material had apparently hit it, cutting into one side of its

Tip for New Writers
One of the strengths of this author's work is the amount of research he puts into every aspect of the technology he uses in a story. Students who find this level of detail intimidating, particularly if they wish to write their own science fiction stories and want to have this quality in their work, can use this trick, borrowed from the screenplay writers for Star Trek. Concentrate on the story's action and characters. When you need a piece of technology, such as the door to an alien craft, simply put a marker to remind yourself, such as "WEIRD DOOR," then proceed with the writing. When you are ready, go back through the story and fill in each of the details you need.

Suggest "...this creature had come from another world..." as a starting point for student stories based on the "what if.." premise of this story.

The protagonist compares the alien to known Earth organisms on many occasions. Discuss with the class if this is simply the author's way of helping the reader see the alien as the author intends, or if this is what any human would do in order to make sense of an alien lifeform. If the latter, what are some possible consequences of drawing such comparisons?

The description of a possible mechanism to move food through the alien's arms is meant to be a replacement for the mechanism of **peristalsis**, as it occurs in the human digestive system. Depending on whether your students are familiar with this mechanism, you may wish to point this out to the class.

Raji is faced with the problem of deciding if the alien being is alive or dead. Elicit from the class the characteristics of living things and have them decide which of these characteristics are the most useful in a first aid situation such as this, where you may not have the same type of organs and physiology.

In case students are curious, spellings such as "centimetre" are retained in this story in all editions of this book because of its setting in Canada.

head; the debris that had likely done the damage was now lying on the floor behind the being's chair. Interestingly, though, the head wound showed no signs of bleeding: the edges of it were jagged but dry.

At first Raji could see nothing that might be a mouth, but then he looked more closely at the middle limbs. In the center of each circular palm was a large opening — perhaps food was drawn in through these. Perhaps the creature flexed its arms after swallowing to move its meals down into the torso.

Assuming, of course, that the alien was still alive. So far, it hadn't moved or reacted to the presence of the two humans in any way.

Raji placed his hand over one of the medial palms, to see if he could detect breath being expelled. Nothing. If the creature still breathed, it wasn't through its mouths. Still, the creature's flesh was warmer than the surrounding air — meaning it was probably warm blooded, and, if dead, hadn't been dead very long.

A thought occurred to Raji. If the breathing orifices weren't on the middle hands, maybe they were on the upper hands. He looked at one of the upper hands, spreading the semi-clenched fingers. The fingers seemed to be jointed in many more places than human fingers were.

Once he'd spread the fingers, he could see that there were holes about a centimetre in diameter in the centre of each palm. Air was indeed alternately being drawn in and expelled through these — Raji could feel that with his own hand.

"It's alive," he said excitedly. As he looked up, he saw the air ambulance hoverjet through the transparent hull, coming in for a landing.

—◦●◦—

The ambulance attendants were a white man named Bancroft and a Native Canadian woman named Cardinal. Raji met them at the entrance to the downed ship.

Bancroft looked absolutely stunned. "Is this — is this what I think it is?"

Raji was grinning from ear to ear. "It is indeed."

"Who's injured?" asked Cardinal.

"The alien pilot," said Raji.

Bancroft's jaw dropped, but Cardinal grinned. "Sounds fascinating." She hustled over to the hoverjet and got a medical kit.

The three of them went inside. Raji led them to the alien; Tina had remained with it. She had the palm of her hand held about five centimetres in front of one of the alien's breathing holes. "Its respiration is quite irregular," she said, "and it's getting more shallow."

Raji looked anxiously at the two ambulance attendants.

"We could give it oxygen ..." suggested Bancroft tentatively.

Raji considered. Oxygen only accounted for 21% of Earth's atmosphere. Nitrogen, which makes up 78%, was almost inert — it was highly unlikely that N_2 was the gas the alien required. Then again, plants took in carbon dioxide and gave off oxygen — perhaps giving it oxygen would be a mistake.

No, thought Raji. No energetic life forms had ever appeared on Earth that breathed carbon dioxide; oxygen was simply a much better gas for animal physiology. It seemed a safe bet that if the alien were indeed gasping, it was O_2 that it was gasping for. He motioned for the ambulance attendants to proceed.

Cardinal got a cylinder of oxygen, and Bancroft moved in to stand near the alien. He held the face mask over one of the alien's palms, and Cardinal opened the valve on the tank.

Raji had been afraid the creature's palm orifices would start spasming, as if coughing at poisonous gas, but they continued to open and close rhythmically. The oxygen, at least, didn't seem to be hurting the being.

"Do you suppose it's cold?" asked Tina.

The creature had naked skin. Raji nodded, and Tina hustled off to get a blanket from her helicopter.

Raji bent over the creature's small head, and gently pried one of its vertical eyelids open. The eye was yellow-gold, shot through with reddish orange veins. It was a relief seeing those — the red colour implied that the blood did indeed transport oxygen using hemoglobin, or a similar iron-containing pigment.

In the centre of the yellow eye was a square pupil. But the pupil didn't contract at all in response to being exposed to light. Either the eye worked differently — and the square pupil certainly suggested it might — or the alien was very deeply unconscious.

"Is it safe to move it?" asked Cardinal.

Raji considered. "I don't know — the head wound worries me. If it's got anything like a human spinal cord, it might end up paralyzed if we moved it improperly." He paused. "What sort of scanning equipment have you got?"

Respiration
The author uses the term respiration interchangeably with breathing. This is likely to present no problem to students as they read the story, but if you are making the distinction between respiration and breathing in your class, you may wish to clarify the meanings.

Possibly new terms for students:
fibre optics - glass or plastic fibres capable of carrying light.
inert - without active chemical or other properties.
LCD - liquid crystal display.

Students can explore the reflex contraction of the pupil to light in the classroom.

The "Standard class-three Deepseer" is a postulated highly advanced medical scanner that plays a vital role in this story as tool for examining the alien's inner structure. Where else would such a device be useful? Have students generate a list of possible applications, medical and non-medical.

Cardinal opened her medical kit. Inside was a device that looked like a flashlight with a large LCD screen mounted at the end opposite the lens. "Standard class-three Deepseer," she said.

"Let's give it a try," said Raji.

Cardinal ran the scanner over the body. Raji stood next to her, looking over her shoulder. The woman pointed to the image. "That dark stuff is bone — or, at least, something as dense as bone," she said. "The skeleton is very complex. We've got around 200 bones, but this thing must have twice that number. And see that? The material where the bones join is darker — meaning it's denser — than the actual bones; I bet these beasties never get arthritis."

"What about organs?"

Cardinal touched a control on her device, and then waved the scanner some more. "That's probably one there. See the outline? And — wait a sec. Yup, see there's another one over here, on the other side that's a mirror image of the first one. Bilateral symmetry."

Raji nodded.

"All of the organs seem to be paired," said Cardinal, as she continued to move the scanner over the body. "That's better than what we've got, of course, assuming they can get by with just one in a pinch. See that one there, inflating and deflating? That must be one of the lungs — you can see the tube that leads up the arm to the breathing hole."

"If all the organs are paired," asked Raji, "does it have two hearts?"

Cardinal frowned, and continued to scan. "I don't see anything that looks like a heart," she said. "Nothing that's pumping or beating, or ..."

Raji quickly checked the respiratory hole that wasn't covered by the oxygen mask. "It is still breathing," he said, with relief. "Its blood must be circulating somehow."

"Maybe it doesn't have any blood," said Bancroft, pointing at the dry head wound.

"No," said Raji. "I looked at its eyes. I could see blood vessels on their surface — and if you've got blood, you've got to make it circulate somehow; otherwise, how do you get the oxygen taken in by the lungs to the various parts of the body?"

"Maybe we should take a blood sample," said Bancroft. "Cardy's scanner can magnify it."

"All right," said Raji.

Bancroft got a syringe out of the medical kit. He felt the alien's hide, and soon found what looked like a distended blood vessel. He pushed the needle in, and pulled the plunger back. The glass cylinder filled with a liquid more orange than red. He then moved the syringe over to the scanner, and put a drop of the alien blood into a testing compartment.

Cardinal operated the scanner controls. An image of alien blood cells appeared on her LCD screen.

"Goodness," she said.

"Incredible," said Raji.

Tina jockeyed for position so that she, too, could see the display. "What?" she said. "What is it?"

"Well, the blood cells are much more elaborate than human blood cells. Our red cells don't even have nuclei, but these ones clearly do — see the dark, peanut-shaped spot there? But they also have cilia — see those hair-like extensions?"

"And that means?" asked Tina.

"It means the blood cells are self-propelled," said Cardinal. "They swim in the blood vessels, instead of being carried along by the current; that's why the creature has no heart. And look at all the different shapes and sizes — there's much more variety here than what's found in our blood."

"Can you analyze the chemical makeup of the blood?" asked Raji.

Cardinal pushed some buttons on the side of her scanner. The display changed to an alphanumeric readout.

"Well," said Cardinal, "just like our blood, the major constituent of the alien's plasma is water. It's a lot saltier than our plasma, though."

"Human blood plasma is a very close match for the chemical composition of Earth's oceans," said Raji to Tina. "Our component cells are still basically aquatic lifeforms — it's just that we carry a miniature ocean around inside us. The alien must come from a world with more salt in its seas."

"The are lots of protein molecules," said Cardinal, "although they're using some amino acids that we don't. And — my goodness, that's a complex molecule."

"What?"

"That one there," she said, pointing to a chemical formula being displayed on her scanner's screen. "It looks like — incredible."

"What?" asked Tina, sounding rather frustrated at being the

distended - def'n. swollen out by pressure from within.

Students who have not yet learned about blood composition or cells may have difficulty with the passages on this page. They will read past them and probably grasp the main point of the story, though missing the significant clues that make the ending reasonable. If you notice some students not enjoying the story or commenting it was confusing, it may be this material.

The Expert Witness
Although each of the characters in this story is presented as having useful skills and knowledge, it is interesting to note that the author has each acting as the "expert witness" to describe or explain some key scientific concept.
- Have students identify examples of this for each character.
- Do all of the "experts" appear equally credible? Why or why not?
- A difficulty writers face when making a character very knowledgeable is how to ensure the character is also likeable. Ask students to find examples of how this author shows the humanity in his experts.

only one with no medical or biological training.

"It's a neurotransmitter," said Raji. "At least, I think it is, judging by its structure. Neurotransmitters are the chemicals that transmit nerve impulses."

"There's lots of it in the blood," said Cardinal, pointing at a figure.

"Can you show me some blood while it's still in the body?" asked Raji.

Cardinal nodded. She pulled a very fine fibre optic out of the side of her scanner, and inserted it into the same distended blood vessel Bancroft had extracted the sample from earlier.

On the scanner's screen, blood cells could be seen moving along in unison.

"They're all going the same way," said Raji. "Even without a heart to pump them along, they're all traveling in the same direction."

"Maybe that's why there are neurotransmitters in the bloodstream," said Bancroft. "The blood cells communicate using them, so that they can move in unison."

"What about the head injury?" asked Tina. "If it's got all that blood, why isn't it bleeding?"

Cardinal moved the scanner up to the alien's small, spherical head. The eyes were still closed. On the LCD screen, the skull was visible beneath the skin, and, beneath the skull, the scanner outlined the organ that was presumably the brain within.

"It's so tiny," said Raji.

Bancroft indicated the spaceship around them. "Well, despite that, it's obviously very advanced intellectually."

"Let's have a look at the wound," said Raji.

Cardinal repositioned the scanner.

"There seem to be valves in the broken blood vessels that have closed off," she said.

Raji turned to Tina. "We've got valves in our veins, to keep blood from flowing backwards. It looks like this creature has valves in both its veins <u>and</u> its arteries." He paused, then turned to Cardinal. "I still don't know if we can or should move the alien."

"Well, the oxygen bottle is almost empty," said Bancroft. "Who knows if it was doing it any good, anyway, but —"

"Oh, God," said Tina. She'd still been holding her hand near one of the respiratory orifices. "It's stopped breathing!"

Arteries or Veins?

Be aware of a potential for student confusion here in the author's reference to arteries and veins. Since earlier in the story, the author states the alien has no detectable heart, the customary distinction of arteries carrying blood to the heart, veins taking it away etc. doesn't apply. It also seems unlikely there would be recognizably distinct structures within various blood vessels to label them as arteries and veins. If any students query the mention of arteries and veins here, remind them that the character is extrapolating from human physiology to try and make sense of something completely new.

Note how the author uses this exchange to tell us a great deal about these characters.

"We could try artificial respiration," said Bancroft.

"You mean blowing into its hands?" said Tina incredulously.

"Sure," said Bancroft. "It might work." He lifted one of the arms, but, as he did so, orange liquid began to spill from the breathing hole.

"Yuck!" said Tina.

Raji pulled back, too. The head wound had started to bleed as well.

"It's bleeding from the mouths, too," said Cardinal, looking at the medial limbs.

"We can't let it die," said Raji. "Do something!"

Bancroft reached into the medical kit and brought out a roll of gauze. He began packing it into the mouth located in the palm of the right medial hand. Cardinal grabbed a larger roll of gauze and tried to stanch the flow from the head.

But it was no good. Orange liquid was seeping out of previously unnoticed orifices in the torso, too, as well as from the soles of the feet.

"It's dying!" said Tina.

Blood was pooling on the spaceship's floor, which was canted at a bit of an angle.

"Maybe one of our viruses has the same effect on it that *Ebola* has on us," said Bancroft.

But Raji shook his head. "Viruses evolve in tandem with their hosts. I find it hard to believe any of our viruses or germs would have any effect on something from another ecosystem."

"Well, then, what's happening to it?" asked Bancroft. And then his eyes went wide. Raji followed Bancroft's gaze.

The orange blood wasn't pooling in the lowest part of the floor. Rather, it was remaining in a puddle in the middle of the floor — and the puddle's edges were rippling visibly. The middle of the pool started to dry up. As the four humans watched, the opening in the middle grew bigger and bigger. But it wasn't round — rather, it had straight edges. Meanwhile, the outside of the puddle was also taking on definite shape, forming straight edges parallel to those on the inside.

"It's — it's a *triangle*," said Tina.

"The orange pigment in the blood — it's probably iron-based," said Raji. "Maybe it's magnetic; maybe the blood is pooling along the field lines formed by magnetic equipment beneath the hull ..."

Interestingly, the author has taken a potentially horrific and threatening scene and, through the reactions of his characters, turned it into one of anxiety for the alien's wellbeing.

But then pairs of liquid arms started extending from the vertices of the central triangle. The four humans watched dumbfounded while the blood continued to move. Suddenly, the six growing arms turned in directions perpendicular to the way they'd previously been expanding.

Finally, the outline was complete: the central object was a right-angle triangle, and off of each face of the triangle was a square.

Suddenly, lines started to cross diagonally through two of the squares — one square was crossed from the lower-left to the upper-right; another from the upper-left to the lower right; and the third —

— the third square was *crosshatched,* as if the patterns from the other squares had been overlain on top of each other.

"The square of the hypotenuse," said Tina, her voice full of wonder, "equals the sum of the squares of the other two sides."

"What?" said Bancroft.

"The Pythagorean Theorem," said Raji, absolutely astonished. "It's a diagram illustrating one of the basic principles of geometry."

"A diagram made by *blood*?" said Bancroft incredulously.

A sudden thought hit Raji. "Can your scanner sequence nucleic acids?" he asked, looking at Cardinal.

"Not quickly."

"Can it compare strands? See if they're the same?"

"Yes, it can do that."

"Compare the nucleic acid from a body cell with that from one of the blood cells."

Cardinal set to work. "They don't match," she said after a few minutes.

"Incredible," said Raji shaking his head.

"What?" said Tina.

"In all Earth lifeforms, the DNA is the same in every cell of the body, including in those blood cells that do contain DNA — non-mammalian red corpuscles, as well as white corpuscles in all types of animals. But the alien's blood doesn't contain the same genetic information as the alien's body."

"So?"

"Don't you see? The blood and the body aren't even related! They're separate lifeforms. *Of course* the body has a tiny brain — it's just a vehicle for the blood. The blood is the

Have students come up with their own demonstration of the Pythagorean Theorem, using materials available in the classroom.

intelligent lifeform, and the body is only a host." Raji pointed at the orange diagram on the floor. "That's what it's telling us, right there, on the floor! It's telling us not to worry about saving the body — we should be trying to save the blood!"

"That must be why the host has built-in valves to shut off cuts," said Cardinal. "If the blood cells collectively form an intelligent creature, obviously that creature wouldn't want to give up part of itself just to clot wounds."

"And when the host dies, the orifices and valves open up, to let the blood escape," said Bancroft. "The host doesn't hate the blood — this isn't an enslavement; it's a partnership."

"What do we do now?" asked Tina.

"Collect all the blood and take it somewhere safe," said Raji. "Then see how much we can communicate with it."

"And then?"

"And then we wait," said Raji, looking up at the transparent ceiling. It was getting dark; soon the stars would be visible. "We wait for other aliens to come and rescue him."

Raji dropped his gaze. The alien blood was forming a new pattern on the floor: the outlines of two large circles, separated by about twenty centimetres of space.

"What's it trying to say?" asked Cardinal.

Lines started to squiggle across the circles. The lines on the right-hand circle seemed random, but suddenly Raji recognized the ones on the left: the coastlines of North America. It was a picture of Earth and of another planet, presumably the alien's home world.

As the four humans watched, the two circles moved closer together, closer still, the gap between them diminishing, until at last they gently touched.

Raji smiled. "I think that means we're going to be friends."

The End

Write your own ending
Have students remove the final sentence from this story and add their own ending. It can be as short or as long as they wish, but I recommend you hold the new ending at three - five more paragraphs. Take up the endings as a class, making a list of how many were upbeat and positive, as the original, and how many took a darker view. Determine, if possible, the most popular new ending, then discuss with the class why they feel this ending was chosen by so many different writers.

Sawyer, Robert J.

Golden Fleece, Warner/Questar (1990)

Far-Seer Berkley/Ace (1992)

Fossil Hunter Ace (1993)

Foreigner Ace (1994)

End of an Era Ace (1994)

The Terminal Experiment (Nebula Award Winner) HarperPrism (1995)

Starplex Ace (1996)

Frameshift Tor (1997)

Illegal Alien Ace (1997)

Factoring Humanity Tor (1998)

Rob's short fiction can be found in science fiction anthologies and magazines, including: *Nebula Awards 31*. He writes a column on science fiction writing for *On Spec*.

The Science of Communication

Rob is the first to admit that he has no post-secondary science background, yet his work is known for its realism and depth of research. The secret is twofold. First, Rob educates himself in every area of science that interests him, reading extensively and talking to scientists. Secondly, whenever Rob requires more information about a particular topic in science for a story, he goes to the source and asks scientists in that field.

Website

See page 118 for a site about Rob's work.

Meet Robert J. Sawyer

"I'm not naturally a writer," Rob admits, which is an odd comment from such a successful author. "I'd rather be with other people," he explains. "I'd like to sit in a street-side café and write in between interesting conversations! But I concentrate best alone."

"It helps to be able to gaze into the distance and think."

Rob balances his need for company and his desire to write. He is active in writers' groups and the science fiction community. He also maintains a busy schedule of speaking engagements. Rob does his writing in the office in his apartment. "There's a great view," he notes. "It helps to be able to gaze into the distance and think."

"...I wanted to be a paleontologist."

Writing wasn't Rob's first choice of career. "In high school, I wanted to be a paleontologist," he recalls. "It's still a passion of mine." Rob discovered that there were few opportunities to work in this field. "My next interest was science fiction. I thought about what would help me become a full-time writer." He considered taking journalism but didn't have the prerequisite courses. "I took Radio and TV scriptwriting instead. It was great. I loved everything, even the hardware!"

At the same time, Rob wrote. "I wrote short stories as well as novels. My first big sale was *Golden Fleece*. I've been making my living as a writer ever since."

Rob lives north of Toronto, Canada with his wife Carolyn Clink. "Carolyn and I met in high school," he pauses and smiles. "Actually, we met in a science fiction club a friend and I started. Not a bad way to find what you have in common!"

Rob's Top Three

"Books I'd recommend? No hesitation. *Ringworld* by Larry Niven. *The Gods Themselves* by Isaac Asimov. And *Beggars in Spain* by Nancy Kress. These are science fiction gold."

What if...

Lesson Suggestions

In 1998, Robert J. Sawyer was elected President of the Science Fiction and Fantasy Writers of America, the foremost international organization of professional writers in these genres, becoming the first non-American to hold this prestigious post. It is a good fit for a writer who has tirelessly and successfully worked to bring science fiction out of the literary basement.

Lesson: Encouraging Creativity

Combine reading this story with your laboratory work on human physiology, particularly pulse and the circulatory system. As a finale, have students work in groups to "construct" a possible alien lifeform, using the worksheet, **Alien Construction** (pg 86), as a guide.

Group

Lesson: Critical Reading Skills

Older students and/or those with experience reading science fiction can accomplish a great deal through the more traditional book report format. This format can also be used to produce a report on this or another short story. Use the worksheet, **SF Book Report** (pg 87) for guidelines. While students can find their own books, you may wish to give them (and the school librarian) the following criteria:

Homework

- The book should be complete in itself, not part of a series (or if it is part of a series, it should be the first book).
- The book should be of a length and prose style the student can manage. (See marginal note.)
- Avoid media tie-ins, such as *Star Trek* or *Star Wars* novels, where the author is constrained to an already developed worldview. (Or, alternatively, have everyone analyze such works and combine with a project on that worldview.)

Lesson: Popular Views of Science and Scientists

- What do people do with the science they learn? This story provides a good passageway into a consideration of careers in science. Have students reread the story and pull out information on the work of each individual. Discuss how science plays a role in each career (you'll have interesting results with the pilot).
- Focus on the medical aspects of science to generate a list of as many careers related to this area as possible. Extend to other types of science. Post these lists in the classroom. If you wish, students can do further research on certain careers

Recommended Materials:
- a copy of the companion anthology, *Packing Fraction and Other Tales of Science & Imagination* per student.
- other materials will vary depending on the chosen activity.

Where to find it:
- If you do not have copies of the student anthology, several of the activities here can be used with other science fiction stories or on their own.
- Consult the list of recommended works starting on page 120.

Build Your Own Alien
There is a design activity on page 69 in which students design an alien lifeform to suit a particular environment. You may wish to combine elements of this activity with the worksheet, *Alien Construction*, on page 86.

Being Realistic
Students doing a book report must be realistic and select a book they can read in the time available. Over and over again, I've seen students who have never read anything longer than a *Goosebumps* choose immense works such as Asimov's *Foundation* or Herbert's *Dune*. Needless to say, they were unable to finish the novels within a reasonable time and so couldn't complete their book reports. They were frustrated, their teacher was disappointed, and the exercise was wasted. The students also developed a firm conviction that science fiction was too difficult for them to read.

living dinosaurs were discovered in Iceland?

Welcome to Europa, Jupiter's Coolest Moon!

An ocean trapped beneath super-chilled ice.

A sun so distant it looks like just another star.

A gravity pull from Jupiter strong enough to crack the ice and let dissolved carbon dioxide explode outward.

Hey. It's home.

To what? What could call a place like Europa home? Exobiologists, scientists who speculate about life on other worlds, are very excited about the chances of finding some form of life on Europa or similar moons. Here's your chance to create your own version, using what you know about life on Earth.

1. Before you begin to design your alien lifeform, make a list of what its body needs to be able to do. Think about what your body accomplishes with its different systems.

2. Think about what you know about Europa. Add to your list any characteristics you feel your alien will need to thrive in this environment. (Hint: You can change or invent one feature of Europa, but it must be something you can reasonably expect.)

3. This is your alien. Add to your list any special characteristics you wish.

4. When your list is complete, construct a scale model of your alien in any medium you wish (or one selected by your teacher.).

Factoids about Europa

- Surface temperature @ - 260°C
- Radius 1565 km (slightly less than Earth's moon)
- Metallic core.
- Images indicate large plates of ice seem to be sliding over a warm interior, much like Earth's continental plates move.
- The subsurface ocean may be warm enough to be slushy or even liquid at lower depths, due to heat generated by the tidal tug of war with Jupiter and its other moons.
- Organic material from comets and meteorites lands on Europa, including a large impact 10-100 million years ago.

(Source: Galileo Research Team Report, NASA)

Alien Construction

Cover Page: Title, Author, Publisher, Year of Publication (first year in print), Place of Publication (country/city)

Synopsis: Summarize the plot of the novel in 100-300 words (a page)

Discussion of Novel

Include the answers to the following in your discussion:

1. Technology Trends

   (a) Describe the scientific or technological trends of today that have been extrapolated in the novel.

   (b) Has the author taken a realistic leap into the new reality described in the novel, or does realism appear to be less important to this author than an interesting story? Support your answer.

2. Moral Lesson: State what you think is the moral lesson that the author wants us to recognize. Support your answer. Also, refer to the author's attitude towards that lesson (pessimistic or optimistic, for example).

3. (a) If your novel describes a future conflict, explain how present society might change to avoid (or better cope with) such conflict.

or (b) If your novel describes significant changes, advances, or extrapolations from current science, explain what changes in our understanding of science would be required to get from the present to the conditions described in the novel.

4. Influences on the Author: Consider the social and scientific surroundings of the author in the time and place when the novel was first published. How do you think these surroundings affected the novel in terms of technology, moral lesson, and the author's attitude?

Conclusion

5. Did the author succeed in convincing you about the setting and plot of the novel. If so, what was most convincing? If not, what would you suggest the author change?

6. Based on your response to this novel, choose one of the following statements about science fiction in general and support it with examples.

   ☐ *Science fiction is a way to test possible future consequences of science on society.*

   ☐ *Science fiction is pure escapism, meant to entertain.*

   ☐ *Science fiction requires more work by the author than a novel set in current society.*

   ☐ *Science fiction requires less work by the author than a novel set in current society.*

SF Book Report

Warm-up

Group

Communicable Disease

Have students read this story, then lead a discussion about the risk of new diseases or disease strains. If your students have learned about AIDS and other diseases, you can have them research incidents of diseases being transmitted by travellers by sea and air, drawing conclusions about the measures which are (or perhaps should be) in place to protect populations. If your students have limited knowledge of disease and disease transmission, you can use this story as part of your introduction to the topic, or simply discuss hygienic measures to prevent the spread of colds and flu.

Group

Additional Lesson Ideas - *Stream of Consciousness*

Lesson: When Understanding Science is Crucial

Most people have listened to a doctor or other medical professional give instructions about their treatment. This information may be crucial to a person's health. Despite efforts by the professional to communicate clearly and well, problems can occur to prevent true understanding in the listener, such as:
• use of specialized language, jargon, or unfamiliar terms;
• reluctance to hear what might be "bad news;"
• fear of revealing they haven't understood.

1. Have students read this story, then ask them to think about a first aid or other medical situation they may have faced in the past in which they had to listen to a medical professional, or in which they were asked to help an older relative interpret what was said.

2. Ask for a show of hands to the following question: "Who is familiar with computers, enough to explain how to do various tasks?" Hopefully, you will have several "experts." Pair each with a partner who is unfamiliar with computers. Have the pairs roleplay a conversation starting with the following question to the "expert," advising the "experts" to use as little jargon as possible.

"How do you copy a file from the hard drive of one computer to the hard drive of another?"

3. Analyze the results as a class. How successful were the "experts" at giving instructions to their "patients?" What problems arose? How did the "patients" feel about the conversations? How confident were they about the information received?

4. Go on to other tasks with the class. After 15 min, ask the "patients" to repeat the instructions on how to copy a file. Discuss with the class what can be done to ensure you do understand the information before leaving the expert.

Lesson: Saying Hello

After reading this story, and possibly others about first contact, have students work in small groups to decide what they would want to say first to an alien visitor and how they might ensure their message would be understood.

What if...

Speculating about Issues in Applied Science & Technology

"...digs all over the universe seemed to look pretty much the same..."

from *Ancient Dreams*
by Josepha Sherman

"Only today's etiquette in their use was missing, manners playing catch-up to technology as usual."

from *Prospect Park*
by Julie E. Czerneda

Larry was particularly struck by the scene in which the Matriarch Acara sets a time limit on the dig when confronted by the young protagonist, Jenna. The brush in the girl's hand is an accurate rendering of an archaeologist's tool. The alien nature of Acara and her importance is emphasized by the gestures she makes against the dual moons. While I've promised not to reveal Larry's surprises, I'd be remiss not to point out the intricate detail on the tablet.

ANCIENT DREAMS

by Josepha Sherman

There were two moons rising in the sky. Otherwise, Jenna thought, brushing stray strands of brown hair back under her sunhat, the vast desert landscape stretching out before her would look just like the North American Southwest on Earth: the same brownish-yellow soil, the same upcroppings of rock and high, flat-topped buttes.

The same heat, too!

The archaeological excavation could have been on Earth as well. At seventeen Earth Standard years, Jenna, accompanying her archaeologist parents, Doctors Ron and Lina Saunders, had already seen a good many digs. And, she thought, digs all over the universe seemed to look pretty much the same, with the area carefully marked off in grids, a pit dug away in equally careful levels, like giant steps, and sweating workers passing up buckets of soil or kneeling with delicate brushes or picks over slowly uncovered artifacts.

The workers all looked pretty ordinary, too. Oh, there were variations, of course. The local folk, the Merediani, had four-fingered hands, and their dark eyes had third eyelids, translucent nictitating membranes that could slide down to shield their vision. But otherwise, like humanoid desert people all over, they tended towards dark hair and dusky reddish skin, which gave them an eerie resemblance to the tribal people of Earth's Southwest. The fact that the atmosphere and gravity were so close to Earth Standard only helped the illusion.

But this wasn't Earth, Jenna reminded herself. This was Meredia, an alien world.

Well, maybe not quite alien. Some of the workers were nodding to her or waving, just like workers on any other site. She recognized Teetkan, a bitter, unemployed weaver who'd found the excavation a much-needed source of income, and Kererat, a laborer willing to put his muscles to any job that paid. There, too, were Regit and Wistan, two wiry young students delighted to have a chance to study their people's past. Regit glanced up at her and grinned as he always did when he saw her. This time he added a very human wink, and Jenna felt herself reddening. He was close enough to human-cute to make her want to giggle like a kid, and he seemed to find her cute, too.

Reading Level
Accessible even to students who experience some difficulty reading. Particularly suitable for those students who have never read science fiction before.

What if...
The author was asked to speculate about future technology, especially that used for communication or discovery. Given her background as an archaeologist, it wasn't surprising the author chose to make a forecast about the future of this field, while at the same time making a statement about the value of maintaining what has been in the past.

Students used to thinking in terms of biology, chemistry, and physics, may not consider archaeology as a science. It is, however, validly considered as such, being both a body of knowledge and a process of inquiry that has in the last few decades become reliant on scientific methodologies and tools, including experimentation wherever possible.

Wistan glanced from his fellow student to Jenna and back again, frowning slightly.

Don't approve, do you? Jenna thought. *You don't approve of anything! Except study. Bet you don't even go partying or whatever else students here do for fun on a night off.*

Not that Wistan — or Regit for that matter — were any of her business. The excavation was the only important thing, and her parents had warned her about getting involved with any Merediani boys.

Not that I would bother with anyone as conceited as Regit anyhow. Or as pedantic as Wistan!

As Regit tried to catch her glance again, Jenna stalked away, pretending to be lost in thought. She and her parents were lucky to get this job; it wasn't going to help anyone if she distracted the workers.

Even if it *was* fun to flirt. And annoy Wistan.

It was easy enough to understand why her parents had been hired. The government officials of New Eretcha, the region's capital city, were a progressive group who had decided that it was time to learn more about their people's past—particularly since New Eretcha stood right beside the mound covering Ancient Eretcha, the legendary city of the equally legendary poet-king, Tarin.

But archaeology was only a dawning science on Meredia, and so the council had looked to outworlders. Now that FTL starship drives had gone from science fiction to fact, permitting really swift and relatively inexpensive travel between planets, it wasn't unusual for off-world archaeologists to be hired by local governments. Ron and Lina Saunders had been eager to work on so famous and mostly undisturbed a site. Understanding a new language and culture quickly wasn't a problem, not with all those subliminal learning programs.

"At the least," Jenna's father had told the council, "we should be able to trace the walls of Tarin's palace. At the best, well, who knows? Maybe we'll find the tomb of Tarin himself."

There were hundreds of stories about the poet-king. Tarin had apparently been a powerful but humane ruler, one who had supported the arts, a true scholar as well as a poet. Assuming that even some of the stories were true, Jenna thought, he must have been a multi-talented genius, like Earth's ancient Egyptian priest-architect-doctor Imhotep or the American President-scientist Thomas Jefferson.

Assuming, of course, that Tarin ever existed! Sure, there are

Willing suspension of disbelief
Faster-than-light travel and the ability to communicate with aliens can be the core of a science fiction story or be, as here, dealt with as a compact between author and reader, a willing suspension of disbelief that allows the crux of the story to proceed without distraction.

the tales, and everyone talks about the EPIC OF GREAT DEEDS he's said to have written, as though it's as wonderful as THE ILIAD — but no one's ever seen a word of it!

Wouldn't it be great if they could find even a piece of pottery with Tarin's name inscribed on it? That was how archaeologists back on Earth had proved the existence of Biblical kings, and the same find just might happen here, lightyears away.

Off-world technology helped, too, with views from space picking out the lines of ancient ruins far more efficiently than from ground level, and with laser sights providing far more accurate measurements. Computers were really useful for dealing with such tedious tasks as sorting potsherds, those hundreds of broken bits of pottery to be found on most sites, by type or size or material. The hard work, though, still had to be done by hand; no machine or computer was sensitive enough to screen through bucket after bucket of soil, hunting for the tiniest scraps of archaeological data.

We're employing a lot of people, like Teetkan, who wouldn't have a coin otherwise.

That didn't mean that everyone here was delighted to see the excavation. Too many of the older or more traditional types had been muttering about "grave robbing" and "desecration." They didn't seem to understand that archaeology nowadays was about extending the knowledge of the past, not about anything as callow as simple treasure hunting!

At least Tarin wasn't a priest on top of everything else. Then we never would have gotten permission to dig!

Unfortunately, someone had recently discovered all about treasure hunting. Lately, things had been mysteriously disappearing from the site, nothing vital or important, since so far nothing vital or important had been uncovered. But small bits of gold or silver had definitely been taken, anything valuable that could easily be sold. It wasn't any of the regular crew, Jenna was sure of that; you went into archaeology for the love of it, not for riches, and they had no reason to destroy their careers so stupidly.

But none of the locals were going to suddenly confess, either. The expedition had posted guards on the site to protect it from any more "mysterious "disappearances," but it wasn't good for the expedition's prestige or anybody's morale to realize there was a thief about.

I guess not everybody holds Tarin in reverence.

Uh-oh, now what was wrong? There was some sort of disturbance on the far side of the excavation workers all over the site

I prefer not to make any assumptions about student knowledge and casually elicit or explain the reference to *The Iliad* during any followup discussion.

If you live in a community where an archaeological dig or finding has raised some controversy, you may wish to have students debate the issue of who should decide whether the search for knowledge such as the one depicted in this story is worth disturbing places held sacred by others.

were putting down their tools to watch. Jenna saw a small figure in a colorful hooded robe standing at the very edge of the pit, arms thrown up and bright amulets glinting, and heard the thin sound of chanting.

Oh, not again! Jenna thought and raced forward.

Only one person wore such amulets and such a robe: the Matriarch Acara. The Matriarch was the ancient and ageless High Priestess of the Powers, and she was a high status person, indeed, the equal of Gerriah, head of the government council. In fact, Jenna thought, if Gerriah hadn't overruled Acara by one vote, the expedition wouldn't be here now. Acara looked on all archaeology as nothing more than graverobbing and all archaeologists as grave robbers.

And yet she's not a bad *person. She means well, I think. She's just so — so hopelessly stubborn!*

As Jenna reached the Matriarch, she heard her father and mother trying their best to reason with the small, determined figure. But, as usual, Acara wasn't allowing herself to hear a thing either of them said.

"Sacrilege," she remarked coolly to the air. "Those who loot the dead will suffer."

It was the calm way she said it that was so chilling. Jenna hurried forward, ignoring her mother's whisper of, "Jenna, no, don't —"

"Let her," her father muttered. "Can't make things worse than they already are."

Jenna licked suddenly dry lips. "Matriarch Acara?"

No answer. Jenna bowed her head politely as she'd seen the locals do. For a long, embarrassing moment, she was sure Acara was going to ignore her. But then a long, four-fingered hand rested briefly on her head.

"Earth Child. You alone are too young to be corrupt."

Jenna glanced sideways at her father, who gave the smallest of shrugs, telling her without words, *we* can't get anywhere with her, see what *you* can do.

"Uh, Matriarch Acara," Jenna began warily, "could we, uh, talk? Away from all the noise?"

The Matriarch hesitated. "Very well, Earth Child. I warn you: If this is about grave robbing, you shall not sway me. But let us hear what you have to say."

Jenna walked with her in silence for a time, out into the desert. *What can I say?* the girl wondered. *What can I possibly say?*

"Matriarch Acara...why do you think my parents are doing anything wrong?"

Acara did not deign to so much as glance at her. "There can be nothing but wrong in the disturbing of the dead."

"Well, uh, I can't argue with that. But that's not what archaeology's all about. It's a science, Matriarch Acara! We aren't grave robbers!"

"I told you I would not speak of this."

"But — but I will. I must. Matriarch Acara, it's not our people who are stealing from the site!"

Now Acara did stop, frowning severely at Jenna from under her hood. "Do you, then, accuse mine?"

"I'm not accusing anyone," Jenna said desperately. "But I know our people! They are devoted to uncovering the — the lessons of the past. They wouldn't..." What would Acara hold important? "They wouldn't debase their honor, not for a mere handful of trinkets."

"That is as it is."

But there was something odd edging Acara's voice, and Jenna said slowly, "This isn't just about the thefts, is it?"

The Matriarch gave a sharp little chuckle. "What, then?"

"Matriarch Acara...are you afraid?"

Acara tensed ever so slightly. "Afraid, child? In the Powers' Names, afraid of what?"

"Afraid that...well...that maybe our dig might find something you don't want to know. Like proof Tarin never existed."

"He did." It was said without the slightest doubt.

"Then why not let us show that to your whole world?"

"By disturbing the dead?"

Jenna fought back a cry of frustration. "It wouldn't be that, not really. I — I've read about Tarin. He was a scholar as well as everything else. I can't believe he wouldn't want his descendants to know the truth about him and his times."

"The child lectures me."

"I don't mean to lecture! But — but back on Earth we had legends about a mighty city, Troy. There's even a wonderful epic about it, THE ILIAD. But for a long time everyone thought the whole thing was nothing but myth. And they would have gone right on thinking that, and a whole chapter of human history would have been lost. But archaeology found the city. Troy really did exist!"

"Your point, child?"

Point out to students who are writing their own stories that the author uses this conversation to tell us a great deal about the protagonist, Jenna. Not only is she quite knowledgeable, but she is willing to stand up for her beliefs even in what must be a very intimidating situation.

"What if...what if we found proof that Tarin really existed? Not just legends, I mean. What if we found real, solid, undeniable proof? Maybe some of his writings — maybe even a copy of the EPIC OF GREAT DEEDS? Wouldn't that be terrific?"

Acara snorted. "'Terrific.' Child, you are a dreamer. I honor that. But I am not persuaded."

"Then you *are* afraid."

Acara held up one slender hand. "Hush. I am not finished. Let your work continue. I permit the passage of three days without hindrance. If, at the end of that time you have found nothing of Tarin, then I shall go before the council and have the work declared unholy tampering." She paused. "Your answer?"

"We can't guarantee finding anything in only three days!"

"Three days, Earth Child. Or none." Acara's hand moved in a clearly ritual gesture. "So shall it be."

Jenna sighed. "So shall it be," she repeated softly.

—◦━●━◦—

"Three days!" Ron Saunders exploded. "Is she insane? We can't —" At his wife's frantic wave, he lowered his voice to a fierce whisper. "She wants to be rid of us, that's all it is!"

"We do still have three days," Jenna reminded him warily. "At least we have that much."

"Useless, just useless!" But then her father ran his hand through his hair as he did when frustrated, and added, "All right. Double time, double wages. We'll get as far as we can before that...that bigoted excuse for a priestess shuts us down."

—◦━●━◦—

Jenna sighed. How long had she been lying in her cot here in her parents' tent trying to sleep? But every time she closed her eyes, she saw Matriarch Acara and heard that implacable voice. Three days. Only three days.

At last Jenna gave up. Quietly dressing so she wouldn't disturb anyone, she slipped outside. The Meredian night was bright, what with both moons in the sky, nearly drowning out the nearby constellations. Jenna craned her head back, trying to make out the unfamiliar patterns of stars. How many times now had she stood under other strange skies? Sometimes she longed for a home base, a home world, friends and parties and all that. But at the same time, she knew she'd miss the excitement of seeing new worlds and helping uncover ancient pasts.

Besides, while the FTL drives allowed quick space travel, they still couldn't eliminate the passage of time. Or times, rather, space time versus that of Earth. If she had stayed behind, she

Many careers in science involve travelling away from home; indeed obtaining higher education in science means leaving home for most students. Jenna's pondering on her own situation thus echoes with what may be going through students' own minds as they begin thinking about their own futures — with the likely exception of worrying about aging *before* their parents.

might well have been an old woman when her parents, still fairly young, returned.

A "psst!" broke into her thoughts. Jenna started, and Regit grinned, his teeth — his very human-like teeth — white in the night. "Don't be afraid," he whispered. "It's only me. Walk with me?"

Why not? Regit wasn't foolish enough to cause any trouble. Besides, he really was cute...and even if he did try anything she couldn't handle, there were guards about. There were, weren't there?

Regit had been murmuring pretty things in her ear, the sort of light nonsense she'd heard from other boys, mostly the sons of Earth ambassadors, on other worlds. Jenna wasn't really listening. "Regit," she whispered suddenly, "something's wrong."

"Nothing's wrong, pretty Earthling, except you're not paying any heed to me."

"Regit, stop it! I'm serious. Where are the guards?"

He stopped, frowning. "That, pretty one, is an excellent question. Wait here."

What if he were the thief? Just because he was cute didn't mean he was honest! "We'll both look," Jenna told him. *And I will keep one eye on you.*

Regit stopped with a hiss at the edge of the excavation. "Look," he whispered. "Asleep! The guards are all asleep."

"Or drugged. Regit, where are you going?"

"The thief's got to be nearby. Maybe I can—"

"Regit! This isn't time to play hero! We have to get the others—"

She was interrupted by Regit's short, startled yelp of pain. Then arms too long and strangely jointed to be human grabbed her. Jenna's parents had made sure she knew self-defense, but she couldn't get a hand free and when she tried to kick, her captor lifted her right off the ground. A four-fingered hand clamped over her mouth before she could scream, but twisting fiercely about, Jenna caught a glimpse of: *Teetkan! He's the thief!*

But the unemployed weaver hadn't been working alone. "Keep her quiet!" a familiar voice hissed. Wistan! Wistan was in on this, too! Jenna twisted again, to catch the edge of Teetkan's hand in her mouth and bit as hard as she could. Teetkan hissed, dropping her, but caught her again, this time about the throat, before she could run or shout for help.

"Why?" Jenna croaked at Wistan.

Suggest "...she might well have been an old woman when her parents, still fairly young, returned." as a starting point or concept for a story.

"Why do you think?" he snapped. "I don't have a name, a famous family behind me."

Tough. A lot of people faced that and didn't turn thief. "And it's not cheap to be a student," Wistan continued. "If I can find treasure, good."

"Very good," Teetkan muttered. "No work in the city. Got to make a living."

Wistan shrugged. "If you had treated your customers fairly, you'd have work. But I'm not interested in your problems. There are higher matters than a full belly. If I can also find something belonging to Tarin — then I'll have something. Be someone."

Be a thief. Great name you'd make for yourself.

But these two were amateur crooks. They shouldn't be wasting time in talking. Jenna went limp the way she'd been taught, and sure enough, Teetkan's grip loosened ever so slightly. Jenna twisted free, delivering a sharp kick to Teetkan's shin. He bent over with a grunt of pain, and Jenna turned to run.

But Wistan caught her by the hair, dragging her painfully back off her feet and —

"Stop!"

The autocratic command rang out like a trumpet. Wistan dropped Jenna, who went flat on her back with a jolt, craning her head frantically about to see who'd shouted.

It was the Matriarch Acara, her small figure all but radiating cold fury. "How dare you desecrate this site?" she cried, her voice pure and clear as ice. "How dare you disturb the dead?"

The noise was finally arousing the whole camp. Jenna saw her parents racing forward among the others, and scrambled to her feet, ready to run. But Wistan also was trying to run. They crashed into each other, and Jenna went flying — right off the edge of the excavation!

I'll break my neck! she thought wildly.

Then she hit — not solid rock or dense-packed soil but something that crunched under the impact —

Ceramic! I've hit a ceramic roof and —

She was falling again, landing with an "oof" in the middle of a chamber heavy with long pent-up air. The others had rushed to the edge of the excavation and Jenna could hear her parents' worried shouts, but for the moment all she could do was sit slowly up and try to catch her breath. She ached from head to foot and there were going to be some beautiful bruises all over, but nothing seemed to be broken. As to where she'd landed...

A tomb. Not the main room, but an antechamber, piled high with clay tablets. Without thinking, Jenna picked one up, seeing an archaic script that triggered the lessons implanted in her brain by the subliminal tapes. She read a little, a little more, and then the sense of what she was seeing sank in so suddenly that she nearly dropped the tablet again. Very, very carefully, she stood and very, very carefully edged her way out of the tomb chamber.

And only then did Jenna shout up to the others: "The EPIC OF GREAT DEEDS! It's down here! I've found part of the EPIC OF GREAT DEEDS!"

Much later, Jenna sat under an awning, her bruises and scrapes treated, watching the busy excavation. There were more guards now, not to deal with the two thieves, who had long since been taken away for trial, but with the crowds of the curious and awestruck. Regit, who had received a nasty blow to the head, was still in the local hospital, but Jenna had been assured he would recover quickly and was already babbling about her heroism.

"Earth Child."

Jenna glanced up, then got to her feet, stiff muscles complaining. "Matriarch Acara."

"No, child. Sit. You have been through much." Acara sat as well, and for a long time neither spoke. Then the matriarch stirred. "Well now. You have fulfilled the vow. Three days — and you found proof, most wondrous proof of Tarin within only one."

Jenna felt herself reddening. "Luck," she said awkwardly.

"Was it? Or was Tarin trying to tell us a message from the past?"

How did Acara mean that? "Then...you will let us continue our work?"

"How could I dare refuse?" Smiling, Acara touched a four-fingered hand to Jenna's head, heart, hand. "So much of value would have been lost if I had won. Come, I am not too old to admit I was mistaken! Is there peace between us, Earth Child?"

Jenna thought of the valuable discovery, of the return to the present of a great work of literature, of the return to these people of their own heritage, and smiled. "There is peace, Matriarch Acara. Oh, there is, indeed."

The End

The preservation of knowledge is still a concern today. While a clay tablet might last for thousands of years, it is unlikely a computer file will remain accessible for as little as five years. (I brought in a LP record once and the class assumed I was holding a laser disc with a movie. When we did a quick survey, there were only two students who were certain they had the equipment at home to play the record.) Discuss this aspect of technology with students. If you wish, start a class display of recording technology. Include samples of older slides and photographs that are starting to lose the blue tones as well as paper beginning to show signs of "foxing" or turning brown and brittle.

Sherman, Josepha

Shining Falcon Avon Books (1989)

Horse of Flame Avon Books (1990)

Castle of Deception: A Bard's Tale Novel, with Mercedes Lackey, Baen Books (1992)

A Strange and Ancient Name Baen Books (1993)

King's Son, Magic's Son Baen Books (1994)

Bardic Choices: A Cast of Corbies with Mercedes Lackey, Baen Books (1994)

The Chaos Gate: A Bard's Tale Novel Baen Books (1994)

The Shattered Oath Baen Books (1995)

Forging the Runes Baen Books (1996)

Son of Darkness Roc Books (1998).

The Captive Soul Warner Aspect (based on the TV Series, *The Highlander*) (1998).

Science Fiction

Vulcan's Forge (1997) and *Vulcan's Heart* (1998) (with Susan Shwartz), Pocket Books (based on *Star Trek*).

Anthologies and Non-Fiction

Once upon a Galaxy August House (1994) (Folktales inspiring modern-day fantasies such as Star Wars.)

Greasy Grimy Gopher Guts: the subversive folklore of children with T.K.F. Weisskopf. August House (1995) (Playground rhymes from across North America)

Merlin's Kin: World Tales of the Hero Magicians August House, (1998).

Magic Hoofbeats Barefoot Books (1998).

Josepha's short fiction appears in numerous anthologies and magazines.

See page 118 for a site about Josepha's work.

Website

Meet Josepha Sherman

"...folklore is part of our human heritage."

Josepha Sherman is a folklorist and former archaeologist as well as an author of fantasy and science fiction. "I have a great respect for storytelling," she comments. "Stories are how we communicate ideas and concepts with one another – and with future generations. The most significant part of being a folklorist is gathering the stories that might otherwise be lost, since folklore is part of our human heritage." She pauses. "And I love the tales for themselves. I enjoy what they say about us, seeing how we're all different—yet all related! I'd love it if my books got a reader intrigued by the world of folklore beyond Disney."

Josepha started writing while an archaeologist. "I haven't exactly left the field, just the museum world. Although a museum is in my newest novel!" What does she bring to her writing besides her knowledge of folklore? She grins. "Curiosity about the world and just about everything in it!"

"I use the Internet all the time..."

Josepha writes anywhere and anytime, but has one distraction. "I use the Internet all the time – talking with other authors and friends, doing research, keeping up with events. You could call me addicted!"

"Events must carry the reader along."

Josepha uses her knowledge of past cultures to enrich the settings of her books. Her stories are also strongly plot- and character-driven. "Events must carry the reader along." She grins. "If you can't stop turning the pages, I'm satisfied."

Josepha's Top Three

"I recommend three classics by Jules Verne. *From the Earth to the Moon*, which includes an impossible launch but some amazingly accurate launch site/splashdown locations, *20,000 Leagues Under the Sea*, which predicts submarine travel, and *Robur the Conqueror*, Verne's take on aviation before the Wright brothers flew."

What if...

Lesson Suggestions

Josepha Sherman is also well known as an editor. Before becoming a full-time author, she worked in a New York publishing house and was responsible for discovering many new talents. She has continued to be a mentor to other writers, on an individual basis as well as through frequent appearances at conventions and other venues. Her other passions include horses of any sort, aircraft, and space.

Lesson: Encouraging Creativity

After reading this story, ask each student to choose a planet or moon from the solar system and imagine they are living on it. Have them design and write a postcard or a travel brochure from their imaginary new home. (Or create a webpage.) The setting and physical details should be as accurate and up-to-date as possible. They should list all sources of information, including any Internet sites. At least 2 of 3 sources must be newer than 1997. (This is because recent interplanetary missions have yielded new information. I like to let students discover this reason for themselves as they go to the literature.)

Lesson: Critical Reading Skills

Have students read the story, then discuss with them how differing goals and opinions need to be considered in decisions about any issue. To bring this point home, choose a science-based issue that impacts on your school and/or community, and have students research as many points of view as possible. Suggest students collect:
- "letters to the editor" from local papers
- articles and editorials
- brochures, posters, and mailings from various interest groups
- government information sheets

Have students examine these publications for viewpoint, source, and treatment of scientific information. Although not all publications will be credible, students should still pay attention to the viewpoints being expressed. Results can be presented in the form of a mock council meeting, a bulletin board display, or as a debate. (See marginal note.)

Lesson: Popular Views of Science and Scientists

To encourage students to think beyond chemistry, biology, and physics, have them look up admission requirements for: archaeology, geology, geography, astronomy, logistics, hydrology, engineering, forensics, anthropology, gerontology, etc.

Getting in touch

If you wish, have students use the worksheet, *A Letter of Concern* (pg 58), to help them write their own letter in response to an issue that interests them.

There are additional lesson ideas on page 113 and 116.

the moon was knocked out of Earth orbit and set free?

When Larry did this illustration, he wanted to ensure a deep, textured feel to the forest, to have it leap out as an entity of its own. To accomplish this, he started in the background and drew in detailed trees, over three hundred in fact, layering each new one on top of those already drawn. If you could push through the trees in this picture, you would literally be faced with more.

Anyone who watched *The Time Tunnel,* an early 70's television series, might recognize Larry's inspiration for the concentric ellipses used to depict the abrupt arrival of the story protagonist in Prospect Park.

Prospect Park

by Julie E. Czerneda

"All right!" The words were punctuated by a fist into the chairarm's upholstery. Tiny motes of dust billowed forth each time. "Go. Go. Hurry! Ah, rats."

"Another missed double play, Mr. Key?"

Peter Key opened his eyes, hastily closing his vidlink to his daughter at first base. He blinked at his secretary, who was standing patiently before his cluttered desk. "He was out. I don't know where they find these umps — " Peter began, then stopped at the slightly glazed expression in the man's eyes. "Right. What do you have for me, Bill?"

"There are several callers stacked in the web for you, Mr. Key," Bill said, folding and unfolding his thin fingers around the web monitor he wore constantly during work. "They actually had to route some to me. I presume you switched your priority mode from business — again?"

Damn right I did, Peter said, but only to himself. Secretaries reported straight to the Director, who unfortunately would take a dim view of the importance of a minor league game, playoffs or not. "Been having trouble with my 'plant, Bill," he said instead. "Thanks for notifying me so promptly." He nodded a dismissal before tapping the end of his right eyebrow. As he accepted the first howling voice in his head, Peter's hand curled as if around the coolness of a baseball.

—◦+●+◦—

"I couldn't reach you at all today, Peter," Lydia's voice was almost as aggrieved as her expression.

"Web was stacked," Peter mumbled around his mouthful of, what was it?, veal. His wife's programming left a bit much to the machinery. He tried to be first in the kitchen, but the day had gone from bad to worse. "I was connected to one supplier after another."

"You need one of those new multi-call 'plants, Peter. I've told you before. It's not good to be out of touch with your family."

Peter opened his mouth to object, but Lydia's righteously upraised forefinger interrupted him. She was connecting to someone on the web. Peter eyed his wife of twenty years with the unworthy thought that nothing could be less appealing than a woman deep in mental conversation, eyes fixed on some distant

Reading Level
Most high school students. You may wish to provide a list of the more specialized terms used in this story to assist ESL and other less experienced readers.

What if...
Cellular phones, faxes, email are all forms of communication technology that are becoming more and more portable — as well as essential to business. The author of this story explores the growing trend to easy access to communication. When is there too much? And why is it so important to us to communicate?

'plant - short for implant

It is the ordinary nature of the characters that comes through in this passage. Even though it is set in the future, it is a future close enough to feel familiar. There are two advantages to this for an author. First, you can use everyday objects and terms, knowing the reader will understand them. Secondly, there is a startling effect that makes the reader focus when you couple something unexpected, such as the implanted communication devices, with something taken for granted, like the feel of a baseball.

"...manners playing catch-up to technology..." is a phrase you can use to explore how society has incorporated acceptable patterns of behavior after the fact into the use of other forms of technology, such as how to answer the phone properly or the rules of the road for drivers.

The author takes care here to show the technology as useful, although annoying to the protagonist. You may wish to ask students about the author's attitude towards new technology as evidenced by these passages. (If I, as author, may oversimplify my attitude, it's all wonderful and I love gadgets as long as there's an off switch available.)

point, chewing overcooked veal.

"How did your game end, kitten?" he whispered to his daughter.

"Shh." Elizabeth, or Bet as she preferred lately, also had a finger up. From her frown, it was an incoming homework assignment. Damn teachers never paid attention to time zones anymore. When he'd been young —

When he'd been young, the implants were already as commonplace and necessary as telephones had been to his parents. Only today's etiquette in their use was missing, manners playing catch-up to technology as usual. Back then, callers could be shut down and ignored. Back then, a family dinner had consisted of those present to smell the food, not every and anyone on the web with a tidbit to share.

Oh, he wasn't a trender, one of those who complained that implanted communication technology was forcing humanity to become animated switching stations. Peter considered himself simply old-fashioned. So what if he switched his priority channel to something he could keep in the back of his mind during dinner, like foreign language opera or bowling replays.

Unfortunately, the new 'plants did away with priorities. All calls were received, and you only had to focus on one in order to interact, like a cocktail party in your head. In his head? Good enough reason not to upgrade, thank you very much.

Peter tried in vain to find some meat a fork could penetrate. "Enough of this," he said out loud and stood, prompting disgusted looks and emphatic fingers from his family members. He waved one hand in apology as he left, heading for his corner of the family room for a peaceful minute alone.

The chair wasn't much — its lumps were in all the wrong spots, a legacy from his mother's side of the family. Still, this was his favorite place in the entire apartment. Both walls were coated with real photographs, twenty-three in all, preserved in plastic. Peter knew each image as if his had been the eyes behind the lens, not his Uncle Thad's. "Prospect Park," Peter sighed to himself, touching the glittering water in the nearest photograph.

Peter reached under the chair and pulled out a thin, metal box, its dents bandaged with wildlife stickers. Peter glanced around to be sure he was alone in the room before hugging the box briefly to his breast.

Some nights, he didn't open the box. Some nights, he switched to the news or to chat mode with friends from work. Some nights, he didn't need to know what was inside.

Tonight, he did. Peter slid the elastic bands from each end, tucking them into his pocket. He had fresh ones ready, but these were still strong. He closed his eyes to savor the moment, only to realize his mistake and open them again to erase the vid image of Brazilian opera.

He was still alone. The lid came off with a slight resistance, as always. Peter rested his gaze on the three items inside, and smiled. A folded brochure, a small cylindrical tool, and an envelope, torn open at one end. Nothing of note, unless you looked closer. Peter took out the brochure.

"Prospect Park!" he read out loud, though he knew all the words by heart. "The Affordable Wilderness Experience!" The pictures echoed some on his walls. Not a person in sight. Guaranteed.

Peter carefully folded the brochure, replacing it in the box. His fingers wrapped around the tool. He examined its knives and files one by one, then pulled out the thin white toothpick and used it to pry a veal remnant from his teeth. "The only gadget Uncle Thad ever needed," he reminded himself smugly.

The useful tool went back into storage, and Peter reached for the envelope. He pulled free its contents, reliving the awe he'd felt the first time. "Paid in Full," he whispered, not needing to see the official script. "One Guaranteed Privacy Zone, Prospect Park, July 24-25, 2056." Only ten years to go.

There was another sheet with his receipt. Peter swallowed as he placed it on top and began to read. The page headed "Be prepared" in lurid red ink was the difference between ordinary camping and the real thing. He'd memorized its exhaustive list of recommended preparations and supplies.

Peter frowned and put the list back in the envelope. So far, all he had was his uncle's tool. There was no money to invest in camping supplies, especially when the trip was a decade away and other needs were closer. Just today, Elizabeth's baseball coach had been after him for tournament fees. And Lydia was doubtless planning to have the new 'plant installed, in herself if not them both.

Thank God, his trip was non-refundable and couldn't be sold to anyone else. Otherwise, he might have been tempted himself, when things were tight. Peter hurriedly closed his box, replaced the elastics (adding two more in case) and tucked it under the chair again.

He leaned back, shifted his back into the most comfortable spot, and rested his eyes on the photograph placed just so. It was

If you wish, ask students what Peter's care of the box tells them about his character. Is the trip or the idea of being able to take the trip more important to this man?

the one that had first called to him. Peter knew every leaf, every stick and mossy stone, every ripple in the dark water where it kissed the shore. That place would someday be his, alone.

—◦—●—◦—

"Key!"

Peter jumped. He hurriedly grabbed for his stylus and pad, dropping both. From under his desk, he said, "Ready, Director Kychuk," before scrambling into his seat and trying to look composed.

Director Kychuk, reigning monarch of Main Street Candies and Sweets financial department, gazed down at Peter Key thoughtfully. "And what you are ready for, Mr. Key?"

"You're here to give me an assignment, sir?" Peter ventured.

The Director accepted the chair Bill wheeled in for him, then waved the secretary out. "Mr. Key," he said in a serious tone. "I'm here to give you something else."

Peter dropped his stylus and pad. "Oh God. I'm fired."

"Of course not!" Director Kychuk looked shocked. "Your work is exemplary, Peter. Most of it. In fact," the man leaned forward in his chair and winked conspiratorially. "You are in line for a promotion!"

"Me?" Peter realized this sounded less than confident and quickly added: "Thank you. Sir."

"And what I'm giving you is the first step — your authorization for a new 'plant. Latest Model. Expenses paid." Another wink. "This one's on us, Mr. Key. We need our top executives to be on-line, all the time!"

—◦—●—◦—

At least he beat Lydia to the kitchen, Peter thought numbly, setting the dials for spaghetti, salad, and, with sudden desperation, an order for wine.

"What's the occasion?" Lydia wrapped her arms around his waist from behind, digging her chin into that shoulder muscle that always tightened up at work. Peter relaxed against her warmth, but kept one eye on supper.

"Director Kychuk's talking about a promotion," he said, absently.

"Peter! That's perfect!" Lydia turned him around with unexpected force, her kiss prompt and enthusiastic. "It's about time they recognized all your work."

Peter decided it was time to ignore dinner. He wrapped his arms around his smiling wife, only to have her upraised finger and shrug come between them. "It's Mother," Lydia mouthed.

The use of the name Main Street Candies and Sweets was purely accidental and not intended to refer to any actual business.

Suggest "..We need our top executives to be on-line, all the time!" as the starting point for stories speculating about business of the future and what might happen if having surgical implants became a job requirement.

One tool a writer uses to show more about a character or situation is in the reactions of secondary characters, as here, where we see how Peter is viewed by his boss and his wife.

"Later."

⸺•⸺

Later was better. Bet was at one of her friends (not all social life could be relegated to webbing). For a wonder, Lydia even set her priority channel to his, something that happened rarely these years. Peter put his worries about the promotion and implant aside, and didn't bother opening his box.

⸺•⸺

White noise. Peter struggled from a dream of blazing light and sound to find it was real. He groped for the control on his eyebrow to connect to the web.

"Peter Key. Peter Key. Peter —"

"Here!"

A burst of information followed: schedules, dates, arrangements. Peter slumped back into his pillow, waiting for the mess to sort itself into meaning. Some problem at work no doubt. But what idiot would use an override signal to reach him? Then some of the information began to organize itself into meaning. Peter sat upright, mouth dry. It was the Park!

⸺•⸺

"When?"

Peter pushed the brochure into one coat pocket, checking that the knife tool was safe in another. "Transport arrives in ten minutes," he said over his shoulder, hurrying to the kitchen.

"They can't do that! You aren't ready." Lydia's panic-stricken voice followed him into the kitchen, like a faint channel on the web. Peter stuffed puddings into his pockets, then added anything else small and portable he could see in the cupboards.

"There's been a cancellation for this weekend," he explained again. "They go through the list until someone can take the trip." He took one look at her worried face and tried to contain his impatience to be gone. "I don't want to wait ten years, Lydia. And this chance might never come again."

"I hope it's worth all this, Peter. And I wish you'd told me," Lydia scolded, but her eyes were wet with tears. "Be careful, wild man," she said softly, doing up the buttons of his coat and finishing with a kiss.

⸺•⸺

Seconds later, the transport alarm sounded. Peter rushed to the access door, waiting impatiently for the all clear on the lock. When it sounded, he entered his passcode, then, hand shaking, entered the newly-authorized destination code for the Park. Any mistakes, and the code would be wiped, his chance gone. No problems. The door whooshed open on the personnel slug. Peter

The trend to be "always in touch" has already begun, as witnessed by the number of cellular phones and notebook computers seen in a quick glance around any rush hour subway car or bus (or on the street). Discuss with students the advantages and disadvantages of this type of access to employees. This can be a good lead into the topic of regulation of technology, since there are many issues from public domain on the Internet to cable TV suppliers which can be used as examples.

Planning to Survive

Despite his years of daydreaming about this trip, it is obvious the protagonist has no idea what camping will be like, as evidenced by the supplies he is grabbing. Many "end of the world" science fiction stories have characters who grab what they can, then must survive. An interesting exercise is to give students five slips of paper. On each, they write down one item they would carry with them if they had to flee their home suddenly (or school) due to some natural (or human-caused) catastrophe. Have all of the slips put into a box. Then, with students in groups of three, have each group pull out five slips. The group must be able to explain how each item will help them survive in the short term or long term. (Allow time for swapping if you wish.) Once all the presentations have been heard, reach a consensus with the class about the most valuable items. (A copy of *"How Things Work"* became a major plot point in one post-apocalypse story.)

Between malls, buses, superstores, and cities with underground walkways, it is becoming possible in some societies to avoid experiencing weather altogether. Yet findings with plants suggest they grow more vigorously if exposed to wind and rain. Have students speculate as to how the trend to protect ourselves from the environment might affect the evolution of some populations of humanity.

Write what you know

While it may seem that science fiction writers rarely follow this advice, in actuality they do. The setting for this story is based on the inner portion of Algonquin Park, Ontario — a favorite camping spot for the author and her family. It is much easier to produce realistic details about places when you've been there. Mind you, not all writers can travel to the scene as Kim Stanley Robinson did for his book *Antarctica*.

smiled one last time at Lydia as he stepped backwards into the protective embrace of the slug's harness. The door closed as his eyes did.

The acceleration and darkness took away all sense of true distance. Within the slug, Peter felt he could have traveled only a few steps down his apartment corridor or across the entire planet. But when the door opened and he was gently if automatically lifted from the slug, it was as if his own world had dissolved around him and reformed into wilderness. He was in the Park! With a sigh, the slug burrowed its way back under the soil, the surface immediately resuming its undisturbed appearance.

The trees were much larger than he'd expected, larger and *moving*. "Of course they're moving," he told himself, "It's windy."

In fact, Peter realized almost instantly, it was more than windy. He'd arrived in the midst of a storm. He tilted his head back, letting the wild courses of rain enter his nostrils and mouth, tasting a metallic tang. Lightning flashed and he closed his eyes. There was only darkness behind his eyelids.

The brochure guaranteed privacy. I may not be connected to the web here, he thought, feeling the need to pose the idea cautiously in a mind so oddly quiet. No opera. No bowling scores. No work. No family.

"Yes!" he shouted, trying to outdo the thunder. Peter shook rain from his hair and laughed.

The next flash of lightning poured light through the forest. Peter quickly took his bearings. Through the trees he spotted the storm-tossed surface of a lake. Closer to hand was a post. "Zone marker," he announced, walking through puddles to put his hand on it. He closed his eyes and pressed his lips against the cold rough wood. No one could transport here until his weekend was over. He was alone!

---◆---

"Well, Uncle Thad," Peter said, chewing on his toothpick, "I'm starting to believe you used a bit more than this on your wilderness travels."

The storm had passed like a magic trick, cued to wash the sky for a sunset glorious enough to bring tears to Peter's eyes. Now he stood in the last of the daylight, his toes dug into the sandy shore, lapped at by idle waves as if the lake were tasting him. Peter's stomach was full of pudding, and he had almost convinced himself to try drinking lake water. But first, he'd have to turn around and face what was coming.

"I'll gather some of the softer branches, make a bed, and sleep under the stars." The plan had sounded better an hour ago, before the darkness snuck under the trees. Peter sighed and turned. He put the tool back in his pocket; its biggest blade was no longer than his little finger and little help against the night.

The forest wasn't totally dark yet. Once his eyes adjusted, Peter could even make out the faint markings of a trail. Feeling on the threshold of adventure, Peter followed it, eyes sharp and ears ready to catch any sound.

The trail led to the privy, the only human artifact tolerated in the Park. Peter refused to be disappointed; he would have had to find it anyway. There were fines against fouling the Park.

Visit done, Peter prepared to follow the trail back. He shivered, realizing his damp clothes were not going to dry in the rapidly cooling night air, but he had no means to make fire. Hopefully tomorrow would be warmer.

A whine in his ear made him jump. Damn web was active again. So much for his guarantee. The whine stopped, started again in his other ear and suddenly multiplied. "Biters," Peter grinned, trying to catch a glimpse of his first wild animals. The little things flew too quickly for a look. Ah, there was one on his hand. Peter watched the mosquito prepare to bite with total fascination.

"Ow!" He slapped it without a thought, then cringed in case the Park authority would suddenly retaliate. Then he was being bitten too rapidly to bother wondering. Hands over most of his face, Peter hurried back down the path.

They were in his ears, his nostrils, nipping through his clothes. He panicked and ran, waving his arms over his head. Suddenly, the ground flipped up to meet him.

— ••◆•• —

Peter woke up, unsure what had happened except that Lydia must have pushed him out of bed. He twisted and tried to push up. Sickening pain shot from his left leg to every part of his body. At the same instant, his hand, which should have been on carpet, slipped on a wet mass of leaves and he fell back down.

It hadn't been a nightmare. He was in the Park, alone, and now he was hurt. Thank God the biters had had their fill of him — unless the cold night air kept them away.

"Broken or sprained, Uncle Thad," Peter whispered, eyes straining in the darkness. He groped for a stick that felt solid enough for his weight, then struggled to rise. He almost fainted but kept trying. The trail had vanished into shadow, but he could

The perils faced in a story don't have to be Earth-shattering to be central to the plot. The accident that turns Peter's trip from uncomfortable to potentially dangerous could happen to anyone — most likely to someone unfamiliar with the terrain.

make out a dim luminescence that might be the lake.

"I'm paying for this. I'm paying for this," Peter muttered to himself over and over as he struggled over slick rocks. He'd learned not to trust logs that felt solid — they usually collapsed when he pushed his stick into them. "They probably lose half their campers this way," he gasped, leaning against a cooperative tree, no longer certain of his direction. "Where do they put the bodies, Uncle Thad?" Peter shook his head. "No bodies. They're loaded for transport to the home code as the next camper's slug arrives. That's the deal."

The thought of Lydia's face if she found his dirt-covered corpse in the access was enough to get Peter moving. He sat on the last big log and somehow pulled his injured leg over it. Abruptly, he was out in the open again.

And the lake waited for him, a dish of black velvet reflecting so many stars Peter could see by their light. A call came from the distance, its throbbing loneliness carving into his soul before it died away. Peter eased himself onto the sand, spellbound.

A line of pale gray rose up through the black sky. Peter puzzled about it for a moment, then caught a whiff of wood smoke. He had a neighbor. For a moment, pain and loneliness made Peter determined to slip into the lake and swim in search of help. Then he slumped back down. "Wouldn't be fair, Uncle Thad," he whispered. "This kind of privacy is once in a lifetime."

—◦➤●◂◦—

Morning brought the loon's cry again, along with drifts of fog hanging just offshore. Peter lifted his face to the first warmth of the sun and thought he might survive after all.

That day was the longest he remembered living. Peter did his best to wrap his leg with pieces cut from his shirt, but touching the bruised, swollen flesh made him nauseous. When his stomach settled, he finished the puddings and sucked on Kool-Aid powder, saving the barbecue sauce packs until he was truly desperate. Different, larger, biters appeared and Peter soon lost any sense of guilt in this kill or be bitten place. He was too hot, and knew he should get out of the sun, but his body remembered the cold night and wouldn't move.

"I'd like to call Lydia, Uncle Thad," Peter said, watching a black insect bury itself in the sand beside him. There were others, evenly spaced, apparently as suicidal. "I need to tell her something. But how?"

His implant was useless. Guaranteed privacy. Well, he'd paid for it. And now he understood why so much of the cost was insurance.

Despite Peter's troubles, he hasn't lost sight of what he wanted from this trip to Prospect Park. If you wish, discuss with students what this adds to their understanding of this character and his society.

The "3 for trouble" code is in place in parks and other areas. It is as low-tech a signal as one could imagine, pointing out how meaningful communication can occur without electronics or even speech.

"A fire would help tonight, if this useless thing could start one." Peter took the knife and, suddenly furious, threw it into the lake. It cut its hole in the water and disappeared.

Three birds flew by and Peter watched them. "Three of anything means trouble, Uncle Thad. You told me that. Put out three, and someone will save me. Well, I paid for privacy — and that includes not being watched, or flown over, or checked on, or —"

Or being saved, Peter finished to himself, calm again. He looked around, feeling he recognized every leaf, every stick and mossy stone, every ripple in the dark water where it kissed the shore. Not a bad place to die.

As long as he could leave a message for Lydia.

—⋅⋅●⋅⋅—

"And you found him here, Ms. Key, right in the access?"

"Yes, Officer. I told you." Lydia could tell by the insurance officer's face that they both knew this was merely a formality. Of course the Park would cover poor Peter's medical expenses. Her husband hadn't regained consciousness yet, but all the specialists agreed he would be fine. His injuries were probably complicated by the shock of being alone. It hit some people that way. Lydia hadn't argued.

The officer had her sign forms, then left. Lydia went to Peter's favorite chair and sat down.

She reached underneath, and pulled out a thin metal box. Carefully, she hugged it to her breasts, then opened it.

The wet torn brochure smelled like pine. Lydia ignored it, and the envelope. Her hand went unerringly to the flat stone she'd found clutched in Peter's hand.

Scratched on it was her name.

The End

What must we say to one another?
In this story, the protagonist, believing himself dying, had to express his love for his wife. Depending on the age of your students, there will likely be some squirming at this concept but I've noticed they do get the point. You may wish to pose this question to students, allowing them to keep their answers private: "If you had to leave tomorrow on an exchange program and could say only one thing to one person, what would you want to say?" (An alternative is to have them think about what they write in friends' yearbooks. Do they usually write something funny or very simple? Since this is a type of time capsule, what could they say instead that could serve as a reminder to their friend years from now?)

Missing: An Expert Witness
Have students identify the "expert witness" in each of the stories presented in *Packing Fraction and Other Tales of Science & Imagination*. They may have trouble with this one. If so, that is because this story relies not on a character, but on a combination of reader knowledge and narration to deliver the necessary science.

Czerneda, Julie E.

Science Fiction

> "First Contact Inc." *First Contact*, ed. Larry Segriff & Martin H. Greenberg DAW Books (1997).

> *A Thousand Words for Stranger*, DAW Books (1997). (Book I in the <u>Trade Pact Universe</u>)

> *Beholder's Eye*, DAW Books (1998).

> *Ties of Power* DAW Books (1999) (Book II in the <u>Trade Pact Universe</u>)

Fantasy

> "'Ware the Sleeper" *Battle Magic*, ed. Larry Segriff & Martin H. Greenberg, DAW Books (1998)

Anthologies

> *Packing Fraction and Other Tales of Science & Imagination*, ed. Trifolium Books Inc. (1998).

Julie's non-fiction titles include numerous science, math, and technology textbooks and teacher resources, as well as the popular *Career Connections* series.

Website

See page 118 for a site about Julie's work.

Meet Julie Czerneda

"I've written for fun since I was about eleven," Julie says.

"But I didn't plan to make a career as a writer." Because she was interested in animals, Julie studied biology, spending several years researching animal communication and evolution. "I'd write science fiction to entertain myself," she recalls. "By university, I was using my stories to play with the concepts I was learning. I always wondered, *what if...*"

When Julie was invited to try writing non-fiction, she had her doubts. "Write a textbook? I was qualified, but I wasn't sure I'd like doing it. But I've always been willing to try new things." Writing and editing texts turned into a successful career, with the added bonus of letting Julie work at home while she and her husband Roger were raising their family.

"I hadn't realized how personal storytelling was..."

Julie kept writing SF for fun, and eventually found the courage to try selling her stories to a publisher. "I hadn't realized how personal storytelling was. The first time someone read the name of my character out loud I blushed. But I was encouraged by other writers I'd met." Having now sold five science fiction novels, Julie is writing fiction fulltime. "It's really too much fun to call a job."

"...science fiction? ... perfect exercise for your imagination."

Julie continues to be active in science education. "Science fiction helps me – and my students — look at science in a different way," she notes. "We think about the wonder of it and the creativity of the people involved, as well as the effects of discoveries on other areas of society." Julie smiles. "Writing and reading science fiction? It's the perfect exercise for your imagination."

Julie's Top Three

"I certainly agree with the other authors' picks, but I'll add C.J. Cherryh's *Pride of Chanur* series, Isaac Asimov's *I, Robot,* and Andre Norton's *Star Rangers* (also sold under the title: *The Last Planet*)."

What if...

Lesson Suggestions

Julie E. Czerneda describes herself as insatiably curious, the sort of person who reads every article in a newspaper and has to see what's over the hill or under rocks. Discovering science fiction was like coming home.

Lesson: Encouraging Creativity
- This story speculated about how people might be affected by advances in communication technology in the near future. *Alternative history* science fiction starts with a "what if..." set in the past, with the author speculating on what might have changed as a result since that time. For example, Andre Norton's *Quest Crosstime* is set in a North America where the Mayan civilization successfully resisted the arrival of Europeans and eventually controlled half of the planet.
- Have students think about a scientific development, issue, or a particular technology that interests them, then use the worksheet, *What if...?* (pg 114), to explore what might happen in an alternate history science fiction story.

Lesson: Critical Reading Skills
As a culminating exercise (or for personal assessment at any time), have students complete the worksheet, *Scientific Literacy Skills* (pg 115). Stress that, like any skills, these are learned and improved through practice. Recommend to students that they get into the habit of reading science, to viewing what they read critically, and to look for answers when they do not have the information they need to make an informed decision about an issue, science-based or otherwise.

Lesson: Popular Views of Science and Scientists
- After students have read this story, emphasize that it was about ordinary people and the impact a scientific development had on their lives. To reinforce the understanding that science is part of everyday life, ask students (at home) to make a list of ten ways in which some aspect of science is affecting their and/or their families' lives. *Homework*
- As a class, combine the lists to produce a survey of science at home. (If time permits, do this as a group activity in which students produce categories and otherwise organize the data.)
- Choose one of the aspects of science at home and speculate on future changes, how these might change people's lives, and how students could find out more. *Group*

While alternative history story-telling can be an excellent way to have students think through possible societal impacts of scientific discoveries and other events, I have observed one small problem with this type of book and younger readers. Some of the books written in this style are so well-researched and plausibly presented that students who don't know their history believe they are reading a novel based on historical fact, rather than the author's speculation. Make sure students understand where the author begins to deviate from known fact.

Drinking from a Box
Older students in high school may not remember but they were likely the first in their families to use drinking boxes routinely. When this new technology for preserving drinks was introduced, it was met with considerable skepticism and sales resistance. It was only as parents found the smaller versions convenient and safe for children that the marketplace opened up. One of the effects has been that parks can now ban glass or metal containers for beverages without causing campers to do without juice, milk, or even wine.

an experimental drill reached the Earth's molten core?

Alternative history science fiction poses this question:
What if something had happened differently?

Such stories look at how life might be today.
What would be the same; what would be different?

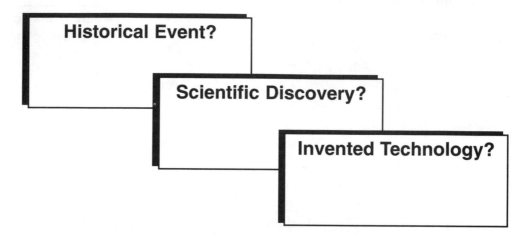

What if...?

1. Decide whether you are interested in "altering" an historical event, a scientific discovery, or an invented technology. Narrow your ideas until you have chosen one specific thing to change in history. For example, you could decide the Roman Empire didn't fall, or that the discovery of gunpowder occurred in North America, or that plastic was invented before paper.

2. From this point on, all elements in your story must reflect this choice. The more ways in which you can depict the "new possibilities" the better. Be as believable as you can. For example, if you decide to alter the past so that alchemists were able to turn lead into gold, would it be reasonable to have people continuing to use gold for currency or jewellery, or would they use it for everyday dishes?

3. To make a story, you need more than an interesting speculation about how the present-day world would change. You need people: characters who are facing some problem or challenge. If you have trouble with this aspect, here are two ways to think about it:

How might people be in conflict with themselves or
their environment because of this change?

How might an individual's life (yours) be affected by
this change?

alternative: def'n. any of two or more possibilities; the freedom or opportunity to choose between two or more things.

Scientific Literacy Skills

Are you a scientifically literate person? Complete the quiz below to find out. (Circle the answer that applies to you.)

1. Can you identify the scientific issues underlying personal and societal decisions?

    Most of the Time   *Sometimes*   *Rarely*

2. Are you able to express your views on those issues in appropriate scientific terms?

    Most of the Time   *Sometimes*   *Rarely*

3. When you evaluate the quality of scientific information, do you consider both its source and the methods used to obtain it?

    Most of the Time   *Sometimes*   *Rarely*

4. Do you feel you make and evaluate arguments based on evidence and apply conclusions from such arguments appropriately?

    Most of the Time   *Sometimes*   *Rarely*

5. (a) Do you ask questions about what makes you curious in everyday life?

    Most of the Time   *Sometimes*   *Rarely*

    (b) Do you determine or find the answers to those questions?

    Most of the Time   *Sometimes*   *Rarely*

6. Do you read and understand articles about science in the popular media?

    Most of the Time   *Sometimes*   *Rarely*

7. Do you discuss with peers the validity of the conclusions in such articles?

    Most of the Time   *Sometimes*   *Rarely*

8. Can you distinguish between what is and what is not a scientific idea?

    Most of the Time   *Sometimes*   *Rarely*

Additional Lesson Ideas - *Ancient Dreams* and *Prospect Park*

Lesson: The Technology of Talk
Use either or both of these stories as an introduction to projects integrating communication or information technology into your science program. One of the features of technology which may be new to students is the design process, in which parameters, sometimes called design constraints, are established first. Any model or design must meet or exceed these requirements. Discuss what these stories say about the need to communicate and share information. From either story, students can produce a list of design constraints for a relevant technology: *Ancient Dreams* - a technology to provide longterm storage of information that wouldn't be lost underground; *Prospect Park* - a technology to provide distance communication without sacrificing privacy.

Lesson: Connecting with the Space Program
To encourage students to learn more about the space program, including the interplanetary missions and the international space station, start by having them read *Ancient Dreams*. Focus their attention on the location, and the need for faster-than-light travel to reach other planets. This can lead into research into the current state of the space program and what is happening within the next few years. You can arrange for your class to communicate with NASA and other space scientists, have a career day linked to the space program, etc. (I've known several physics teachers who delight in challenging students to design their own space craft and describe how it would move in space. This can be a whole topic in itself.)

Lesson: Ecological Thinking
If you are planning an ecology unit and want to try a different way of bringing interrelationships home, use *Prospect Park*. This story shows the main character existing in two seemingly unrelated ecosystems, an underground city and coniferous forest. After students read the story, have them identify as many components of each ecosystem as possible. Write each component on the board so that you end up with two lists separated by enough space for their answers to: "how these ecosystems connected?" If you wish, ask which could exist alone, leading to the idea that cities are dependent.

Website

See page 118 for some sites regarding space.

Elementary science classes were invited to help NASA investigate the effects of spaceflight on canola seeds. Interested teachers were sent seeds, instructions, and equipment to run the comparative growth experiments. Results were pooled and posted. There is a website on page 118 showing one school's experience with this project.

What if...

Annotated List of Science Fiction Resources

Non-Fiction

The following titles contain excellent information on authors and their works, including thoughtful presentations on the interplay between science fiction and society.

Clute, John. (1995) *The Illustrated Encyclopedia of Science Fiction*. MacMillan Toronto Canada (Wonderful resource. Highly recommended.)

Clute, John & Grant, John (ed.).(1998) *The Encyclopedia of Fantasy* Orbit, St. Martin's Press (Contains references to the distinction between the genres.)

Grolier, *The Science Fiction Encyclopedia*, CD-ROM (A wealth of accessible information, ideal for student research)

Silverberg, Robert. (1998) *Reflections and Refractions: Thoughts on Science-Fiction, Science and Other Matters*. Underwood Books.

van Belkom, Edo. (1998) *Northern dreamers: Interviews with Famous Science Fiction, Fantasy, and Horror Writers*. Quarry Press, Kingston, Canada. (Good information on the career of writing as well as authors.)

The following titles focus on specific areas of science fiction:

Bova, Ben, with Lewis, Anthony R. (1998) *Space Travel*, Writer's Digest Books.

Fenner, Cathy & Fenner, Arnie (ed.) with Jim Loehr. (1998) *Spectrum IV: The Best in Contemporary Fantastic Art*. Underwood Books.

Hanley, Richard. (1997) *The Metaphysics of Star Trek*. Basic Books NY. (a philosopher's analysis of the science and philosophies presented in the television series. Well-written and organized, with index.)

Hartwell, David G. & Cramer, Kathryn (ed.). *The Ascent of Wonder: The Evolution of Hard Science Fiction* Tor Books

Nicholls, Peter. (1984) *The World of Fantastic Films: An Illustrated Survey*. Dodd, Mead & Company.

SETI Institute. (1995) *The Rise of Intelligence and Culture*. Teachers Ideas Press. (Part of a set of 3 teacher resources, "The SETI Academy Planet Project," containing dozens of great activities concerning the possibility of life on other worlds, including science fiction activities.)

Solow, Herbert, F. & Justman, Robert H. (1996) *Inside Star Trek: The Real Story*. Pocket Books. (a behind-the-scenes look at how the series came to be produced as well as details about the series.)

Strick, Philip. (1976) *Science Fiction Movies*. Octopus. (Although an older title, it is frequently available in libraries and recommended.)

One of the foremost science fiction literature collections in the world is the Toronto Public Library's Merril Collection of Science Fiction, Speculation and Fantasy. Contact the Merril Collection for suggested titles and for help with research into authors, etc.

List Updates

This list is meant as a starting point and is in no way all-inclusive. I'm sure I've missed many useful and important works. There is a simple reason for this: with the exception of a couple of the reference works which came highly recommended by individuals working in this field, I've included only those titles I can vouch for personally — and I can only read so much. To offset this problem, this list is available on my website. I will be adding new titles to it as they come to my attention, so please visit. There is also a submission form on the site to allow readers to recommendations for this list, so if you are aware of a book or other title I should have, please let me know.

Website   http://www.transdata.ca/~czerneda

Magazines of Interest

Reviews and other information about the science fiction field can be found in several publications, including:

- *Locus: The Newspaper of the Science Fiction Field*
- *The New York Review of Science Fiction*
- *Science-Fiction Studies*
- *Science Fiction Chronicle*
- *Parsec*
- *On-Spec*
- *Odyssey*
- *Northern Fusion*
- *Starlog Magazine*

Website   See page 118 for some non-fiction sites.

Website

These links were last verified October 1998.

Website Updates

As everyone use the Internet soon learns, websites either last indefinitely or are gone the moment after you save them. The sites in this book were stable at publication, but please refer to my own website links page for updates and corrections as they occur. (I also highly recommend using a generalized search engine such as http://www.dogpile.com when students search for authors.)

Website

http://www.transdata.ca/~czerneda

Sites I've Found

_____

_____

_____

_____

_____

_____

_____

_____

_____

_____

_____

Websites

Authors in this book with sites

Czerneda, Julie E.
http://www.sff.net/people/Julie.Czerneda (archive)
http://www.transdata.ca/~czerneda (updates)

Sawyer, Robert J.
http://www.sfwriter.com

Sheffield, Charles
http://www.sff.net/people/sheffield/

Sherman, Josepha
http://www.sff.net/people/Josepha.Sherman

Science Fiction Resources

http://www.clark.net/pub/iz/Books/Top100/top100.html
One of the better organized "top 100 science fiction" lists.

http://www.starrigger.net/#books
A list of science fiction titles, organized by reading level.

http://www.mid-ga.com/sff/authors.html
Links to science fiction authors and reviews.

http://www.sfsite.com/
Information about science fiction and authors.

http://www.magicdragon.com/UltimateSF/SF-Index.html
5 000 links to science fiction-related sites, including authors.

http://www.sfwa.org/links/booklink.htm#reviews
This is a list of science fiction specialty bookstores, with their links, so you can find one near your location.

http://www.starflight-reader.com/
A web magazine about science fiction and fantasy with reviews of new work and useful links to conventions etc.

Science Fiction in the Classroom

http://www.kenyon.edu/depts/biology/bio3/bio03syl.htm
"Biology in Science Fiction" synopsis, showing how this university uses science fiction as a vehicle to teach biology.

http://merlin.alfred.edu/degraff/sf.astro/
Using science fiction as part of a course in science & astronomy.

What if...

http://home.interlynx.net/~chbray/index.htm
One school's results for classroom-linked project with NASA investigating the growth of seeds which had been in space.

http://www.kithrup.com/brin/
Reading for the Future Project: a campaign aimed at using science fiction literature to help improve literacy, with links.

http://tommy.jsc.nasa.gov/%7Ewoodfill/SPACEED/SEHHT ML/scifi.html
Teacher resources from NASA on using SF in the classroom.

http://libnt1.lib.uoguelph.ca/SFBib/index.htm
Science Fiction and Fantasy annotated reading list for educators, compiled by the University of Guelph library.

Of Interest to Writers and Artists

http://www.icomm.ca/onspec/sflinks.htm
Canadian science fiction links, including awards.

http://www.sfsite.com/analog/
longest continuously published sf magazine

http://www.sfsite.com/asimovs/
Asimov's SF mag

http://www.scifi.com/sfw/
SFW primarily covers news and reviews, but also carries some of the best digital "cover" art on the 'Net and has a monthly column written by SF critic and scholar John Clute.

http://www.sfcentral.com/vanmeter/A3_home.html
This is the site for an sf artist with links to art associations of interest.

Science Resources

http://www.newton.cam.ac.uk/newtlife.html
Excellent site about Sir Isaac Newton

http://wwwcn.cern.ch/~mcnab/n/T/
This is another site about Newton, but more tongue-in-cheek. It contains poetry by scientists about Newton and his work, among other things.

http://www.jpl.nasa.gov/directory/
The ultimate site to start researching any topic on space.

Website

These links were last verified October 1998.

Sites I've Found

_____

_____

_____

_____

_____

_____

_____

_____

_____

_____

_____

_____

_____

_____

_____

_____

_____

_____

_____

_____

there were only 100 years until our sun went nova?

What's missing?

Don't see authors such as Isaac Asimov, Robert Heinlein, Arthur C. Clarke, and Ursula LeGuin in this list? This is because I've found books by these and other classic, well-known authors in almost every school library. Many teachers are familiar with their work. And to be honest, some, not all, of the classics won't work well with today's young reader. So this space is for perhaps lesser-known works, for books and authors I've found to be successful in the classroom. There are many I've missed, but then there are only so many pages in any book. Please check my website for a constantly expanding version of this list.

Website http://www.transdata.ca/~czerneda

Where to find it:

- libraries (interschool loans)
- specialty science fiction bookstores*
- on-line bookstores
- solicit donations of books from the school community
- request copies from the publisher
- garage sales and second-hand bookstores
- request copies from the author (for short fiction, ask permission to copy for class use)
- book exchanges

* One way to update your school library's collection is to trade. For example, I've been in libraries where they unknowingly have copies of early science fiction languishing on the shelf, worth hundreds of dollars each to collectors but hardly ever read because they appear "too old." In trade to a specialty store, the library can replace these titles with newer editions, as well as purchase additional books.

Fiction

Recommended Authors

The following authors have a large body of work in print or otherwise available, so rather than list all of their titles, I have made general comments below:

Bujold, Lois McMaster. Any and all of her works. Some mature themes, so better suited to high school libraries, but accessible to most readers. The Miles Vorkosigan character in several books is physically challenged yet utterly believable as a hero. Readable and fast-paced.

Cherryh, C.J. Any and all. Highly recommended. However, her work can be a challenge to poorer readers. Those starting to read this author might like to begin with the *Chanur* series.

Norton, Andre. Any and all of her works. A feature of this author is that many of her protagonists are young people, finding their own identity or talent. Accessible to most readers. Highly recommended. *Beast Master* was one of the first SF novels with a North American protagonist. She is a Grand Master and has hundreds of titles in print.

Specific Titles for Any Reader

Card, Orson Scott. (1985) *Ender's Game.* A prodigy at strategy games is trained to fight a future war. Highly recommended.

Carver, Jeffrey A. *Dragonrigger.* An imaginative and convincing portrayal of possible star flight.

Hopkinson, Nalo. (1998) *Brown Girl in the Ring.* Warner Aspect. Although there are fantasy elements, this book deals with issues surrounding organ donors as well as the survival of the human spirit despite the collapse of a city's infrastructure. Highly recommended. (There are a couple of passages which are fairly gruesome. These are almost medical in nature and the students I had read them were not bothered at all.)

MacAvoy, R.A. (1983) *Tea with the Black Dragon.* Bantam. Combines charm, high-tech theft, and a man who may be a dragon searching for truth in a lovely, readable (and not long) book. Highly recommended.

McCaffrey, Anne. (1969). *The Ship Who Sang.* Ballantine Books. This popular and prolific author will have many books in school and public libraries. The best science fiction title, in my opinion, is this one about a future in which ships and even cities are controlled through the thoughts of physically challenged yet brilliant individuals.

McIntyre, Vonda. (1989) *Starfarers*. Ace Books. A brilliant tale of how humanity might succeed at interstellar flight.

McIntyre, Vonda. (1997) *The Moon and the Sun*. Pocket Books. (See also *The Dreamsnake*) Strong science concepts with very nice characterization.

Moon, Elizabeth. (1996). *Remnant Population*. Baen Books. This is a well-crafted first contact novel, told from the perspective of an older woman who wants to be left alone

Niven, Larry, Pournelle, Jerry, & Flynn, Michael. (1991). *Fallen Angel*. All of these authors have extensive bodies of work. This particular book, about a future where part of the Earth is in an ice age, America is anti-technology, and space stations must steal supplies, just works especially well when looking at science with students.

Sawyer, Robert J. (1994) *End of an Era* Ace Books. This is a time-travel adventure that involves a nice treatment of scientists as well as dinosaurs.

Sawyer, Robert J. (1995) *The Terminal Experiment* Harper-Prism. The author includes newspaper headlines and articles to evoke the reaction of society to the scientific changes taking place in the story.

Specific Titles for Better Readers

Gardner, James Alan (1997) *Commitment Hour*. Avon Eos. This is an interesting story about what might happen if humans were biologically altered so that they altered sex each year from birth, then at twenty had to choose one sex to remain.

Herbert, Frank (1965). *Dune*. This book can often be found as a paperback in libraries, a rarity among "classic" sf authors, and many students are amazingly familiar with the characters from the popularity of the related computer game. The first book in the series, it also is considered the best. Highly recommended but formidable in length. Not a good choice for a book report.

Kress, Nancy. (1988). *An Alien Light*. Arbor House. This author's work is extraordinary, and this is just one of the titles I'd recommend highly. Because it deals with many aspects of learning, it's particularly meaningful to use in schools.

McKillip, Patricia. (1987) *Fool's Run*. Warner Books. This is a hard science fiction work by an author better known for her lyrical fantasy. The language is still lyrical (and the protagonists are musicians), but the setting is an orbital penal colony in a gritty realistic future. Highly recommended.

Censorship Issues

With the exception of a very sincere if loud gentleman attending a booksigning, who insisted there was no further need to write books because the only book necessary had already been written (begging the point of why he was in a bookstore to start with), I've had no problems concerning the use of science fiction. I only recommend works I would read myself — perhaps a form of censorship, but if so, at least I'm saving someone with similar tastes time and aggravation.

Science fiction, by its nature, has always been a literature willing to push at the edges of society, to confront, to poke holes in conventions, and to accept differences among individuals. For this reason, many of its finest works are bound to offend somebody, sometime. There is also some very poor writing out there called science fiction whose claim to readership is based more on shock than plot.

My only recommendation regarding censorship is this: if you are providing or recommending books to students, use your best judgement as an educator. When in doubt, and you don't have time to read the material first yourself, simply choose another book.

Magazines

Here are some of the magazines carrying short science fiction:

- *The Magazine of Fantasy & Science Fiction*
- *Asimov's Science Fiction*
- *Interzone*
- *Science Fiction Age*
- *Odyssey* (United Kingdom)
- *Analog*

Keep track of the following:
- science fiction stories, novels, and films that work well in class;
- possible mentors and speakers;
- authors whose style and approach suit your students (both fiction and non-fiction);
- websites, both new and updates to existing bookmarks;
- contests;
- conventions;
- events such as national book days which may allow you to further promote scientific literacy.

Tesseracts is an annual anthology of Canadian science fiction, fantasy, and horror, both short fiction and verse. New editors are selected each year and submissions are in English or French (translated for publication). A selection of these anthologies will provide a broad cross-section from which to choose, but are recommended for older students.

Recommended Movies
As models for use of science or portrayals of scientists:
- *Contact*
- *Blade Runner*
- *2001: A Space Odyssey*
- *Gattaca*
- *Aliens*
- *Terminator 2: Judgement Day*
- *Close Encounters of the Third Kind*
- *White Dwarf*
- *The Andromeda Strain*
- *Jurassic Park*
- *Twister*

As examples of plot construction and other story-telling techniques:
- *The Fifth Element*
- *Men in Black*
- *Star Wars*
- *War of the Worlds*

Also of interest
- *Lawnmower Man*
- Any *Godzilla* or early *Blob* movie

Stirling, S.M. (1997) *Island in the Sea of Time*. Roc Books. For more mature readers. Intensely researched and well-presented alternate history. The present-day island of Nantucket is sent back into the Bronze Age and its inhabitants must cope.

Vinge, Joan. (1980) *The Snow Queen* and its sequel *The Summer Queen*. Questar. The underlying premise is that of a world that gains then loses its connection to an interstellar empire for centuries at a time. It's a wonderfully complex and well-developed story. Highly recommended.

Anthologies

Quality short stories can be most easily found in any of the annual "best of the year" collections, variously titled as:

The Science Fiction Hall of Fame
Best of the Nebulas (selected by their peers)
The Hugo Winners (selected by peers and readers)

Dubois, Gardner (ed). *The Year's Best Science Fiction: Fourteenth Annual Collection*. St. Martin's.

Hartwell, David (ed) (1998) *Year's Best SF 2*. Tor Books.

There are also "themed" anthologies, such as those below. These are very useful if you wish to have students work within a similar theme, or when comparing the different viewpoints of authors. I've used the following with students:

Greenberg, Martin H. & Thomsen, Brian (ed.) (1998) *The Reel Stuff*. DAW Books Inc. NY. (Collection of award-winning science fiction stories that were the source material for famous films.)

Greenberg, Martin H. & Segriff, Larry (ed.) (1997) *First Contact* DAW Books Inc. NY (Collection based on the moment humans met aliens.)

Greenberg, Martin H. & Segriff, Larry (ed.) (1996) *Future Net* DAW Books Inc. NY (Collection based on 'net technology.)

Hartwell, David, & Grant, Glenn. (1994) *Northern Stars: The Anthology of Canadian Science Fiction*. Tor Books. As well as science fiction stories, this book contains essays, author interivews, and references to awards and other aspects of Canadian science fiction.

"Second star to the right...and straight on 'til morning."

Peter Pan

What if...